April's Breeze

Hope you enjoy this story and it creates a desire to learn more about the "ordinary" people who created our nation.

Gary Entwistle 10/17/22

GARY ENTWISTLE

gcentwistle@icloud.com

Copyright © 2022 Gary Entwistle
All rights reserved
First Edition

PAGE PUBLISHING
Conneaut Lake, PA

First originally published by Page Publishing 2022

ISBN 978-1-6624-8050-8 (pbk)
ISBN 978-1-6624-8051-5 (digital)

Printed in the United States of America

INTRODUCTION

By the rude bridge that arched the flood
Their flag to April's breeze unfurled.
Here once the embattled farmers stood
And fired the shot heard round the world.

—Ralph Waldo Emerson,
Concord Hymn

This is the opening stanza of the poem Emerson wrote for the 1837 dedication of the Obelisk commemorating the battle at Concord's North Bridge on April 19, 1775; this battle signaled the outbreak of the American Revolution. These lines are also inscribed on the base of the Daniel Chester French Minuteman statue across the bridge. The legacies of many of our Founders—with names like Adams, Franklin, Jefferson and Washington—germinated and blossomed during these trying years; this story centers around some lesser-known participants of the American Revolution and the impact the war had on their lives. Throughout history, wars and conflicts have interrupted daily life, sometimes temporarily, often permanently, many times tragically.

This is a love story, enveloped in war and amid the birth of a nation. It is a tale that symbolizes the sacrifice, devotion, and commitment of heroic, ordinary people. It reflects deep loyalty and eternal hope while describing an impassioned rebellion. The experiences of the men and women portrayed on these pages are repeated too often across the world and over many generations.

INTRODUCTION

The characters in this story—mostly real, a few imagined—embody the human spirit of people who desired and fought for the basic freedoms they felt they deserved. Most of the book is based on historical facts, people, and places; inner feelings, fears, and hopes described, as well as private conversations, are from inferences based on common human emotions and behavior that would be expected in the context of the given situation. Where historical data was not available, some literary license was taken to fill gaps and create a neatly woven tapestry of events. The actual historical material is simply the backdrop for the human drama taking place.

The inspiration for this book came out of a love of history and the stories often hidden among names, places, and dates; it was also inspired by an interest in the human history often lost in world-changing events. The "shot heard round the world" is well-known; lesser known are the lives and love of Lydia Mulliken of Lexington and Dr. Samuel Prescott of Concord. Their story embodies the pain, hardships, sacrifice—and spirit—of so many people who were there and helped bring this country to life.

PART 1

On the Path to Revolution

Chapter 1

April 10, 1775
Early morning

Faster and faster, the bay mare galloped through the newly plowed field, her reddish-brown coat shimmering in the early morning light and her black mane and tail flowing in the breeze. The wind tugged and pulled at the tricorn hat of the rider, but the hat held on stubbornly. The rapid and rhythmic pounding of the hoofs broke the early morning silence. Clumps of soil from the field were tossed up behind the horse as she moved rapidly on her course.

In the distance, a solitary white building and grey barn appeared to grow larger as the rider approached. A trail of smoke curled out of the stone fireplace chimney. The barn on the left still shielded the rising sun, as a woman waved frantically from the back corner of the barn.

"Dr. Prescott! Thank the Lord you came so quickly! Come here. Isaac is on this side. He fell and has hurt his leg badly!" the woman cried.

"Whoa, Duchess," said the rider, bringing the horse to a quick stop. He removed a leather pouch from his saddle bag then tied the horse's reins to a white fence next to the barn. Almost six feet tall, the man had neatly trimmed light-brown hair and a clean-shaven face that matched his pleasant presence. He put his tricorn hat on a fence post, turned to the woman, and said, "Be calm, Sarah. I'll take care of Isaac."

CHAPTER 1

Dr. Samuel Prescott of Concord had come to the aid of Isaac Walker and his family many times in his few years as a doctor, going back to when he apprenticed under his own physician father, Abel Sr., and then being mentored by two older brothers, Benjamin and Abel Jr. While only twenty-three, he was already a seasoned and respected doctor in the area. The Prescott family lived just outside the center of Concord, a bustling town of about 1,500 people, sixteen miles northwest of Boston, while the Walkers' farm was some distance west. Samuel had been there many times assisting in their care for illnesses and injuries. He remembered the first time, asked to accompany his father, when a large stone had rolled over Isaac's foot while he was moving it from the field. Then one additional visit this last spring with Abel Jr. when Isaac cut himself while sharpening an axe.

"Isaac, what have you done now?" asked Dr. Prescott as he walked around the rear of the barn. He had been at the Walkers' farm just three months earlier during the winter when Isaac fell on some ice walking to the barn.

"Doc, I think I broke my leg. I fell off the ladder while trying to fix a missing shingle. My right leg gave way as I tried to stand and get back up, so we sent my son, Jacob, to get you."

Just as he finished speaking, a boy on an old brown horse rushed around the corner of the barn.

"Father, are you all right?" he shouted.

"Don't worry, Jacob. He'll be fine." Samuel started working on the man's leg.

"I tried to keep up with you but couldn't," said the boy. "Your horse is so fast!"

"Duchess knows the back roads and fields as well as I do." Dr. Prescott laughed. "You did a fine job getting to our house so quickly. I'm glad I was in our barn when you came looking for me."

Using a knife from his pouch, the doctor cut back the leg of Isaac's trousers and felt around the area on Isaac's right shin to check his tibia. He could feel a section that felt displaced, but it appeared to be a simple break. Samuel decided he could shift the bone back into place, and if secured, it would heal. He knew Isaac was a tough New

England farmer but also knew there would be a lot of pain when he set the bone back in place. He placed a small hickory stick from his bag between Isaac's teeth.

"Bite on this when I tell you," Samuel told his patient.

"Now!" Grabbing the man's leg, the doctor shifted the bone back into place. Isaac groaned, and Dr. Prescott could see him clenching his fists tightly, but he tried to lay still. Samuel lined leather splints on either side of the leg, tying it in place with some clean white cloth strips. He wrapped the entire section of leg with a piece of leather from his bag, which he then tied in three places: one at the top, one in the center, and one at the bottom.

"Jacob, help me move your father into the house," Samuel called. Together, they carried Mr. Walker into the farmhouse and laid him on his bed in the rear room.

"You'll have to stay here for a while," Samuel instructed. "Jacob and Sarah will take care of the farm for a few days. I'll be back to check on you."

"Are you crazy?" asked Isaac. "It is almost planting season, and I need to get the fields ready."

"I understand that, Isaac. But if you don't let that heal properly, you'll suffer with it all summer."

Isaac groaned, but nodded his agreement.

As Samuel prepared to leave, he quietly whispered to Sarah, "I told him a few days, but it could be weeks before his leg is strong enough. Make sure he lies still and send Jacob for me if Isaac gets a fever or the leg swells. I'll be back later in the week to check on him."

Sarah said, "Thank you, Dr. Prescott. We'll keep an eye on him." Then, whispering, she asked, "What is being said in town regarding the tensions in the colony? While at church on Sunday, I heard many of the women murmuring about the militia preparing to defend the town."

Prescott shook his head. "I don't pay much attention to it, Sarah. I'm from a family of healers, not soldiers. We try to concentrate on the physical health of our neighbors and let others deal with the politics. To be honest, though, with the Provincial Congress meeting in town, there have been many such discussions, both among the

CHAPTER 1

Loyalists in town and those who are unhappy with the king's treatment of our colonies. I will try to find out more for you."

"Please let us know if you hear anything ominous, as Isaac is concerned," she answered.

When Samuel went back outside, he pulled Jacob aside. "Your father will be needing your help. How old are you now?"

"I just turned thirteen, Doctor Prescott," Jacob replied, standing tall and sticking out his chest. "I can do anything on this farm that Father needs done."

"Let me know if you find that you need help. There are plenty of men in town who would be glad to assist. Make your father proud," Samuel said, patting him on the side of his shoulder. "I knew he could count on you."

Samuel packed up his bag, took his hat off the fence post, mounted Duchess, and waved as he departed. He glanced at the farm as he left, thinking how he would enjoy having a similar property to share with a certain young lady who occupied his thoughts on his way home.

Chapter 2

April 14, 1775
Early morning

A warm glow from the crackling fire in the fireplace filled the room of the old house just east of the center of Lexington. This was a village of eight hundred people, about halfway between Concord and Boston, made up of sprawling fields lined with stone walls. Typical for a New England village, it had a town common surrounded by houses, a tavern, and a meetinghouse where the Sunday services were held. The old house was like many of the older homes in the village with dark-brown clapboards, aged by the weather and time, and a center stone fireplace. Next to the house was a small structure with a faded wooden sign hanging in front, showing a clock face and the name "N. Mulliken, Clocks" on top. Inside the house, the pleasant fragrance of burning oak and maple drifted into each room. The early morning light filtered through the windows, leaving shadows on the back wall. A young woman stirred the boiling contents of a large pot, adding a little water, then some more items from a wooden bowl as she stirred the mixture.

"Good morning, Lydia. Did you sleep well?" asked an older woman entering the room and wrapping herself in a worn woolen blanket that was draped over a large spinning wheel. She tucked her long, dark-brown hair with gray streaks into a bonnet and lit a candle on the windowsill before lighting a lantern on the table.

"Good morning, Mother. Yes, I slept very well but was up early, so I've started breakfast for all of us."

CHAPTER 2

"I'll wake your brothers Nathaniel and John so they can get more wood for you. The firewood bin is rather low."

Mrs. Mulliken (whose name was also Lydia) went to a side room to wake her oldest sons. Since their father's passing eight years earlier, they had been the "men of the house." They slept downstairs, near the door to guard the house and family.

"Nathaniel! John! Time to get up. Lydia needs some wood, and the house needs warming."

John rolled over and pulled a heavy blanket over his head, mumbling, "Lydia's a big girl. She can get her own wood."

"Let's go, John!" Nathaniel, the older of the two brothers, scolded him, pulling the blanket away and throwing it on the floor. "It's our responsibility. If you had brought in more wood last night, there would have been enough this morning." Nathaniel was the oldest male in the family and tried to keep them all in line to keep the household operating smoothly.

He slipped on his trousers and socks, grabbed his boots from the corner, and pulled on a heavy coat that was hanging on a wooden peg on the wall in the hallway. Dressed, Nathaniel entered the main room of the house.

"Sorry, Lydia. We'll get more wood," Nathaniel said to his sister. Slightly taller than his sister's average height, his dark, curly hair and short beard made him appear older than his twenty-three years. Although two years older than Lydia, Nathaniel considered them equal partners in helping their mother run the household. He often spent the rest of his time continuing his late father's clock shop in the adjoining structure while Lydia helped her mother and older sister, Mary, with the chores and youngest children.

"Thank you, Nathaniel." Lydia smiled at her brother. She saw how hard he worked every day and his attention to detail and knew that he took his responsibilities very seriously. With the mixing of ingredients completed, she pushed the pot crane back into the fireplace, returning the porridge to the heat.

Nathaniel pushed back his hair and put on his tricorn hat. He then headed outside to the woodshed just as John stumbled into the main room. John was just a little shorter than his brother; he had lighter, straighter hair, pulled back and tied with a clip, and a smooth face that made him appear younger than twenty. He went outside to help Nathaniel. Upstairs, the sounds of the other children waking could be heard. The two youngest, Rebeckah at thirteen and Joseph at nine, were assisted by oldest sister, Mary. She helped them get dressed then gather their heavy woolen blankets and quilts and place them back on their beds. Once they were ready, Mary hurried down to help Lydia. As the oldest of the seven children at twenty-four, Mary knew her time was coming to take over the household, especially with Lydia talking about a wedding coming in the next year.

Mrs. Mulliken helped the younger children wash while Lydia and Mary put wooden bowls, pewter dishes, and mugs on the old wooden table. Nathaniel and John returned with armfuls of firewood, placing them next to the fireplace. The older boys then sat at the two ends of the table. Mrs. Mulliken poured porridge into the bowls, and they waited for Lydia to sit.

Lydia was adding another log to the fire before joining them to eat. As she did, a big piece of burning maple in the fireplace suddenly split, throwing out a large red ember that landed on the hem of her skirt. Rebeckah and Joseph, the two youngest, jumped up from the table, screaming, and ran toward the door.

"Watch out, Lydia!" yelled John. The flames began spreading along the edge of her skirt, with smoke filling the room. John rushed to her side and extinguished the smoldering skirt she was wearing by stomping on it with his boot several times then pouring some water on it from a pitcher that was on the table

"That was close! Your entire skirt could have caught on fire, spread onto the wooden floor and furniture, and caused the whole house to burn down! Are you all right?"

"Yes, thank you, John. I am fine. This house has lasted nearly a hundred years. I don't think one more spark will hurt it."

"Well, if John lives here much longer, the house won't make another hundred." their other brother, Samuel, eighteen, laughed as he helped Rebeckah move her chair closer to the table. "He's almost caused four fires in the past week."

CHAPTER 2

They all liked teasing John, which was easy to do as he always seemed to be in trouble for something. He was the second oldest son, two years older than Samuel was, but all the brothers were very close. Samuel preferred that his siblings call him Sam, as it made him feel closer in age to his big brothers. It was the name Rebeckah had always called him when she was younger.

Changing the subject, John asked Lydia, "I heard you mention last night that we might have company this week. Is *your* Samuel still coming for supper on Tuesday?" He hoped, by directing everyone's attention to Lydia, they would leave him alone.

"Yes, he'll be here after dark. Will you and Nathaniel be back?"

Nathaniel responded, "We're leaving Monday morning to drop off a clock for Dr. Warren in Boston, set it up, and get another ready for drop off in Salem on Tuesday morning. We should be back in plenty of time. I'm looking forward to seeing Samuel again. Haven't spoken to him for a while."

They all sat quietly for a few minutes, trying to finish their breakfast. Once they were done, Mary took Rebeckah and Joseph outside while the others cleaned the table.

Mrs. Mulliken asked Lydia, "Are you and Samuel going to discuss details for the wedding while he is here?"

"One of the reasons Samuel is coming is to do that, and to officially get Nathaniel's approval," answered Lydia. Turning to her brother, she said, "He has a lot of respect for you, Nathaniel. Since you are both the same age, he knows all of the responsibilities you handle, and he wants to show you that respect by getting your approval."

Nathaniel put his arm around his sister's shoulder. "If there was anyone who I would give my sister to, it would be Samuel Prescott. Even if he *is* from *Concord*. There are a lot of fine men here in town, but you had to fall in love with a doctor from that elite town." He was just teasing her, laughed and kissed her on the forehead, then went to the clock shop with John.

They only had two days to finish the clock they were building for Dr. Joseph Warren, a well-known physician and political leader in Boston. He had promised his militia leader, Captain John Parker, that he would question Dr. Warren on activities of the king's forces in Boston. There was a pile of wood that needed to be cut, sanded, and stained, and the clock mechanism had to be fitted into the face properly. Nathaniel and John went to work, each with a specific task that needed to be finished. Nathaniel's specialty was the clock mechanism and engraving while John excelled at cabinet making and the trim. They worked quietly together all day to complete the clock.

Chapter 3

April 15, 1775
Dawn

The mist and fog hanging over Boston Harbor that early Saturday morning had finally started to lift, melted away, and cleared by the rising morning sun. The sun's light as it rose peeked through the leaded glass windows of the home on Charles Street, slowly creeping across the floor, up the footboard of the bed, and across the quilts and blankets until it reached his eyes. Major John Pitcairn of the Royal Marines was normally an early riser and was surprised to be awakened by the sun. He had been up late the night before, revisiting plans detailing a change in routine for the king's troops that was to be further discussed this day with General Thomas Gage, military governor of the Massachusetts colony, and the other commanding officers. Pitcairn typically spent his nights in the barracks with his men, but he had spent the past two nights at the home of a Loyalist to keep the plans secret.

He yawned, stretched, and rose, ready to face the day ahead. After dressing, he gathered his notes and sat at a table near the window with his breakfast, lighting a lantern for added light. He removed some notepaper and an envelope from a drawer beneath the table, dipped a quill pen in the inkwell, and started to write.

My dearest Betty,

Not a day passes without you being in my thoughts. As we plan our next actions against the rebels and scoundrels creating mischief in this colony, I wanted to reassure you that your devoted husband and two sons are in good health. I see our son William regularly as he drills with Marines, but I have little contact with Thomas and his army regiment.

We all look forward to the eventual day we will return to your side and are safe at home.

Hoping this finds you well, and with deepest affection.

Your loving John

Pitcairn carefully placed the letter in the envelope, addressed it, and added it to a small pile of correspondence he had set aside for his aide to process. Then he reached down and lifted a cloth bag that was lying next to the table and unfolded a white towel, revealing two silver pistols. They had rams' heads with curved horns at the butt end, and his initials were engraved on the sides into elaborate floral scrollwork. These were precious to him; they had been given to him by a former superior officer while he was in London. He regularly cleaned and polished them, keeping them in good order for when they would be needed. When finished, he wrapped them up again, slid them back into the bag, ready to be put into his saddlebag when he departed. Rising from his chair, Pitcairn walked to the corner where his coat was hanging on a wooden peg. He slipped it on carefully, adjusted the collar, and stood in front of a long mirror to inspect himself. There were very few men who better represented the dignity, honor, and elegance of the royal military. The scarlet coat with the black trim and gold roping, overlapping his white ruffled shirt and white vest, over his white trousers, added to the grace, class, and dignity of this much-admired man, an officer well respected by his men

CHAPTER 3

and colleagues, and even among the local townspeople. During his time in Boston, he had become an active attendee at the Old North Church, near the barracks. This provided him with some friendly interaction with the people of the city and kept him attuned to the needs of Loyalists as well as those opposed to actions of the Crown. He was considered a tough disciplinarian by all but was also judged to be very fair, even in disputes between the soldiers and citizens.

Satisfied that his uniform was proper and complete, Pitcairn rolled up the plans and headed downstairs to meet with General Gage and the others.

"Good morning, Major," shouted his aide as he reached the bottom of the stairs. "The general is waiting for you."

"Thank you, Hastings. I have left some letters and notes on my table. Can you be sure they are sent today?"

His aide nodded and went to get the papers.

Major Pitcairn walked into the large room where General Gage was waiting. The general was back in Boston years after returning to England from the colonies following the end of the Seven Years' War with his American wife, Margaret. He had been assigned to restore order to the chaos enveloping Boston after a band of rebels had thrown 342 chests of tea into the harbor sixteen months earlier in December 1773, protesting the tax imposed on them by Parliament, with martial law then being imposed. This was what the colonists saw as the latest in a succession of punitive measures applied by a government in which they had no representation or voice. All the other officers had not yet arrived as General Gage wanted time to speak with Major Pitcairn alone first. He saw John entering the room and stood to greet him.

"Major, it is a pleasure to see you," said General Gage. "Are your accommodations acceptable?"

"Yes, General, for now," answered the major. "I understand the need to be close to you and your staff for this important matter, but much prefer staying in the barracks near my soldiers. We have had some issues with them buying rum from the colonials that has caused some health problems, so I want to keep an eye on it."

The general nodded. "Understood. In the meantime, were you able to review the recommended actions we discussed?"

"Yes, General. They seem sufficient for my Marines. If we need to have the other units preparing for some type of mission, it is best to alter their duties. Are you concerned with recent activity of the colonial militias?"

General Gage rubbed his forehead and told him, "I had sent out some scouts in March to get an idea of the current attitudes of the provincials and received worrisome information regarding storage of large amounts of weapons, including cannons, in towns west of here. Loyalists in the Concord area have continually provided details of military stores being gathered. This information was shared with certain people who have contact with the Crown. Yesterday I received direct orders from Lord Dartmouth with instructions from the king that we are to send a sizable force to Concord, seize and destroy any weapons, and if possible, arrest and make an example of any of the rebel leaders. We have information that John Hancock and Samuel Adams will be in Lexington over the next few days after finishing provincial meetings in Concord."

"Adams is a troublemaker and scoundrel," said Major Pitcairn. "We would be well served making him quiet. And I wouldn't be concerned about venturing out into the countryside. My impression of most of these rabble rousers is that they will back down at the first sign of force from our army. If we use force, it should be considerable, but I believe if I even start pulling my sword from its scabbard they will run away!"

"No one knows about these orders but you. I shared concerns with my wife last night as she is from the colonies and seems to have a better understanding of their concerns and reasons for causing us such trouble. She constantly scolds me not to be the instrument in the sacrifice of colonial lives. I will be letting the other officers know what they need to do with their men, but the actual mission objectives will be revealed once they are on the way." He turned to look out the window. "I don't trust the people in this city. They have too many ears to the ground and seem to know what we are doing before we do."

CHAPTER 3

"Who will be leading your mission?" asked John.

"Colonel Francis Smith, with you leading the advance guard. Your Marines won't be needed, as the light infantry will be used for their speed and agility and the grenadiers for their strength and size. I need your help leading the other companies, as you are respected by the men and I don't have as much faith in all of the other officers. Smith seems to know the terrain better than some of our other officers as well."

As they were talking, Pitcairn heard the other officers arriving outside. "I will keep this to myself, General."

As the other officers entered the discussion, General Gage informed them that several units would be marching out of the city sometime in the next couple of days.

Lord Percy, one of his leading officers, was glad to hear the news. "About time, General! You have been a bit lenient with the ruffians, and we need to show them that we mean business."

One of the other officers raised some doubts. "Sir, are we sure we want to venture into the countryside, knowing the attitudes of the provincials at this time? Are we not making ourselves more vulnerable?"

Major Pitcairn spoke up. "These people are a lot of noise, but no substance."

General Gage agreed. "The entire region of provincials is made up of nothing but bullies with Boston having the biggest of them. We must stand up to them for once."

The officers nodded and laughed. However, one of them offered a word of caution. "Do not take these provincials lightly. Many of them fought alongside us in the Seven Years' War and are capable military men and leaders."

John Pitcairn shrugged. "In the year I have been stationed here in Boston, I have seen nothing to frighten me about their ability to fight our troops. They are undisciplined and ill-equipped against our forces."

"When do we proceed with this excursion, General?" asked one of the junior officers.

"Tuesday night. We will transport the troops over to the Charlestown side and march west from there. Do not inform your men yet. We want this to be a surprise. It will be more effective. Have them ready so they can march before midnight. Colonel Smith will provide more details tomorrow." General Gage rolled up his plans.

"We should send out some patrols before we depart, watching for any couriers who notice our activity and possibly provide some advance warning to the towns," suggested Major Pitcairn.

"You have my approval," replied General Gage, nodding and returning to his desk.

The officers left, each returning to their respective units and preparing their junior officers for the upcoming mission.

Chapter 4

April 15, 1775
Late afternoon

Samuel let Duchess trot along at her own pace, returning home from patient visits; up ahead, he saw his older brother, Abel, coming onto Lexington Road and heading toward the center of town.

"Abel!" he shouted. "Wait up. I'll join you."

Samuel unbridled Duchess, gave her some water and turned her into the barn, then joined his brother for the half mile walk to the center of town.

"Where were you headed?" Samuel asked.

"Wright's Tavern. I saw Amos Melvin and David Suttle earlier. They both said they were tired of plowing fields and wanted to talk."

Young Dr. Prescott was always amused that Wright's Tavern could be busy at any time of day. A large, barn-red building with black shutters and doors, the tavern had four chimneys and was located next to the meetinghouse in the center of town. It was a common place for friends and neighbors to gather. The air inside the tavern was full of fragrances from drinks and foods being prepared in the kitchen. It was usually dark inside, even during the day, as the tall but narrow windows provided little light; there were many candles and lanterns inside. Samuel and Abel sat at their favorite table near the fireplace, asking tavernkeeper Amos Wright to bring them some mugs of flip—a mixture of eggs, sugar, and rum. Soon after they arrived, they were joined by friends, Amos and David.

"Thanks for meeting with us," said David. "Been a tough couple of weeks getting my fields ready for spring, and I just needed to get away for a while."

Amos Melvin agreed. "I have been pulling up large stones from my field all season, and I think I've added thirty feet onto the length of my stone wall."

"We are always glad to have a chance to just talk," Abel said, and Samuel nodded.

As often happened when the young men were together, the young ladies of Concord were the topic of conversation.

"So, Abel, when are you going to find a prize like your brother, Samuel, has? Miss Mulliken is far superior to anyone in this town," Amos stated.

"Amos, you know I think Lydia is very special, and I'm glad my brother was able to earn her affection. I have my mind on someone of my own…"

David rolled his eyes. "Not Abigail Temple? Do you still consider yourself worthy of her after she dismissed you so rudely after service last Sunday?"

"Actually, it's her sister, Anna, who interests me. Even though she has been ill, she is always glad to smile whenever I approach."

David turned to Samuel and asked, "Samuel, you're both doctors. Don't you have anything in your medical bags for this lovesick fool?"

They all laughed. When they returned to their discussions, it took on a darker side as they turned to politics. Amos related some news they had not previously heard among the rumors in town.

"I was asked by our militia commander, Major Buttrick, to assist in moving some munitions in town. The major had received word from Dr. Warren in Boston that Loyalist spies here in Concord had discovered supplies that we were storing. Several men were brought to Colonel James Barrett's farm on the other side of town, where there were four cannons hidden. John Hancock, while attending the Provincial Congress meetings here, notified the Committee of Safety that recent activities in the city might indicate a mission to find and destroy the cannons, as well as seize any other weapons and supplies.

CHAPTER 4

We moved the cannons, barrels of flints, musket balls, and powder to Groton and Stow. I also volunteered to be on watch as needed and sound the alarm with the meetinghouse bell if we heard of any Royal Army activity."

"I'm telling you, Amos, those armed bullies have no right to be here, trying to intimidate us. They should just go back to England or someplace else where they are needed." David shook his head in disgust.

"Actually, it's comforting having them here," Abel replied, with a smirk on his face. "Keeps us safe knowing we're protected by the best army in the world. A toast to General Gage and his troops!"

They all laughed at his false sense of gratitude and pretended to toast, lifting their pewter mugs into the air.

"It's not that funny." A voice from a table in the rear corner of the tavern interrupted their moment of levity. An older man, with a long, slender, red scar on his right cheek, stood up as he spoke. "Out here, in the towns and villages, you don't deal with them every day. They're not constantly looking over your shoulders, watching your every move."

Samuel responded. "Pardon me, sir, but I don't believe we've made your acquaintance."

"John Masters, sirs. I work the docks in Boston, mostly Griffin's Wharf. Just passing through on my way west. Time to find new work."

They all nodded politely, acknowledging his introduction. Samuel stood and offered his hand, but the man ignored the gesture before he continued. "I had to get out of there. Since that night five years ago, I've dreaded every day around those swine."

Samuel, Abel, and their friends looked around, unsure what they were about to hear and wondering who was in the tavern that might overhear the discussion. Many of the other people in Wright's had stopped to listen, the tavern becoming very quiet.

"Five years ago? What happened then?" asked David.

"Do you mean the massacre?" asked Abel. "Surely, you weren't there."

"Aye, my young friend, March 5. It was a horrible night and an experience I won't soon forget."

"Tell us about it, John," Samuel said.

"I was out with some men I worked with, and we encountered a mob who were harassing one of the guards at the Custom House. It happens often, as many of the unemployed have nothing better to do than bother the soldiers, whom they blame for Boston's worries. Since the Quartering Act ten years ago, the citizens of Boston have felt imposed upon, and the anger, fear, and hatred have been building. Usually, there is some shouting and yelling, and everyone goes on their way. On that night, though, it blew up."

He took off an old worn hat and wiped his sweaty brow. Picking up a mug of ale, he drank it quickly and continued. "In my years on the docks, I've had many a fight. Sometimes you need to vent your anger, right, lads? But this was different. As the anger and fear boiled over, some of the people in the mob started throwing snowballs and sticks at the sentry. He yelled for help, and reinforcements gathered around him. One of the reinforcement soldiers hit someone with the butt end of his musket to back him off, then one of the people in the mob hit the soldier with a club. Suddenly, unexpectedly, shots rang out. I was horrified as the men in front of me were struck in the head with musket balls, including Crispus Attucks and James Caldwell, friends of mine. Other men also fell before the crowd started to run away and an officer got the soldiers under control. Five men died, one only seventeen years old. The soldiers were as stunned as the crowd, but at that moment, seeing the blood of fellow Bostonians flowing red on the cobblestone street, splattered on the snow, I felt true hatred. Although I had never trusted the soldiers, I honestly thought they would never shoot innocent people, even if provoked. Now I know they will."

Reuben Brown, who owned a harness shop in town, joined the conversation. "I fear more of that is ready to happen," he said. "With the Provincial Congress finishing their meeting here in town, rumors have it that something is going to happen soon."

CHAPTER 4

"The Regulars won't leave the safety and comfort of Boston," Amos said with scorn. "They have no reason to come out into the countryside and confront any of the tension that might be building."

"I fear otherwise," Reuben argued. "Whether to arrest colonial leaders, break up the Congress, or just to send a message to all of us, some type of strong action will be taken."

"And that action will involve bloodshed," added John Masters. "Hear my concerns, for the army has been hungry for battle. Many people in town resent the Parliament continuing to impose more taxes on us than citizens in England, including that Tea Act, giving the East India Company a monopoly in the colonies. Since the port was closed after we turned the harbor into a giant teapot in protest a year ago this past December, tensions have risen. Gage and his bullies think they own the city. And his soldiers feel the tension too, waiting for some action. But be aware, they are cold and ruthless."

Samuel was surprised at the tone the discussion had taken. While he, too, had heard rumblings of concern in the community, he did not realize how serious this had become. He was uneasy with the tension and the suddenly somber mood in the tavern.

"Surely, you're overreacting," he said, hoping for some reassurance.

"My friend, we have reports of discussions overheard by stable boys within the city that many of the officers believe a quick, sudden strike by the army, including burning of some villages, will put an end to any talk of rebellion." Masters pounded his fist on the table. "Many of the officers doubt the resolve and even courage of the local militias. Trust me—the city, maybe the colony, is ready to explode. All it will take is someone to light the fuse."

"Samuel, I have heard this as well in Menotomy and Charlestown while visiting patients this past week. One of my patients was actually melting pewter dishes to make musket balls as I was visiting," Abel said. "I didn't think much of it at the time."

Amos added, "Many of us have living relatives who came to this country seeking liberties that are now in danger of being taken away by force if we don't stand up for ourselves and our families."

David reminded them that even Reverend William Emerson had spoken of the fear of attack by the Regulars at his last sermon. "Remember, he said that there was an approaching storm of war and bloodshed."

"And he practices what he preaches," said Reuben. "He is an active member of our militia. Although a man of God, he passionately believes in self-determination and a man's freedom from tyranny."

As though it had been planned, Reverend Emerson walked into the tavern, looking for Amos Melvin.

"Amos, my good man, are you still available to provide the watch at the meetinghouse this week?" asked the reverend.

"Yes, I am," responded Amos. "If there are any alarm bells needed, Reverend, I will be ready. But can you do me a favor and speak to Martha Moulton? Let her know I will be there. She is always protecting the meetinghouse and doesn't trust anyone being there without her knowledge." Martha Moulton was a seventy-one-year-old widow who lived near the meetinghouse.

"Of course. She just likes to keep an eye on it as a good neighbor. I'll tell her you have my permission to be there."

"Thanks, Reverend," Amos replied. "Please, join us for a mead or cider."

"Thank you, men, but my wife, Phebe, is outside in serious discussion with several of the parish women. I think I need to rescue her." He tipped his hat, bowed, and left.

Samuel decided it was best to also leave. He stood up, patted Reuben Brown on the shoulder, and said goodbye to his friends. "Come on, Abel. Let's head home before it gets too late." As they left, they heard many of the men continue the discussion.

Heading out of the center of town, Abel asked him, "Samuel, why did we leave? Don't you want to know more?"

"Of course, I do," Samuel answered. "But I will talk to Nathaniel Tuesday night during supper at the Mulliken house. He's a member of the Lexington militia, and he will have a better understanding of all of this. His commander, Captain John Parker, is very respected in their town and probably has shared all he knows with his men. Their pastor, Reverend Jonas Clarke, has also been preaching to his

CHAPTER 4

parishioners that they have rights and need to defend those rights. Nathaniel can give me some idea what he has heard and if anything is being discussed in Lexington. Better than getting frightened by a bunch of drunks, right?"

He gave Abel a quick shove, and Abel shoved him back, then put his arm around his younger brother as they both laughed. They waved to Reverend Emerson and his wife, who were talking to Martha Moulton in front of her house. The brothers made their way down Lexington Road, pleasantly greeting several townspeople along the way. Most people appeared to be living their life as though nothing was happening, just shopping or spending time with friends and family.

Chapter 5

April 17, 1775
Midday

The old wagon creaked and rattled as it slowly made its way over the gravel roads between Lexington and Boston. Earlier that morning, Nathaniel and John had packed up the clock made for Dr. Joseph Warren, and they were taking it to his home to be set up, assembled, and turned on. Nathaniel was eager to talk to the doctor after hearing some rumblings in town about possible troop movements in the city; he knew the doctor would have the latest news. Dr. Warren was well-known throughout the colony for his beliefs in the rights of the people in Massachusetts and beyond. Nathaniel had seen him present a moving and emotional tribute at the second anniversary of the Boston Massacre three years earlier.

They crossed over Boston Neck—the only access to the peninsula which housed the city, surrounded by the harbor and the mouth of the Charles River. The city was bustling with activity as they made their way down Tremont Street, turning onto Hanover Street and approaching Dr. Warren's house. As Nathaniel brought the team of horses to a halt, a very distinguished and elegant woman came out of the door, covering her head with a shawl and quickly disappearing down a side alley. Nathaniel looked at John quizzically, shrugged his shoulders, and they climbed off the wagon.

As they uncovered the clock in the back of the wagon and carefully removed the pieces and stood them against the side of the house, Dr. Warren opened the door.

CHAPTER 5

"Nathaniel, John, so good to see you. Right on time, as promised. I am truly looking forward to having this fine clock for my entryway."

"We know you will find it functions well and are pleased you chose us to create it for you," said Nathaniel. "Can you show us where it needs to go? We will get it ready."

"Follow me," the doctor said, leading them down the hall. At the end was a wide wall between two doors leading into adjacent rooms. "Here, this is where I would like it to stand."

"Perfect," John said. "We will carry it in and have it running shortly."

They went back outside, carried in the movement that was wrapped carefully for the trip, and placed it on the floor. Then they carried in some odd pieces before lifting the main body of the clock and very delicately moving it into place. It stood nearly seven feet tall and had a round face with *Nath'l Mulliken* and *Lexington* engraved on a copper plate above the numbers. They installed the movement, added some trim and hardware, used the key to wind the movement, and set the weights and pendulum into operation. It was a handsome piece made of finely finished cherry wood, with round finials on the top corners and an eagle perched proudly in the center.

"Splendid!" exclaimed Doctor Warren. "It exceeds my expectations. What a magnificent work of art."

"Thank you, sir. Our father trained us well," Nathaniel said as he shook the doctor's hand.

Dr. Warren went into a side room and came back with an envelope of currency. Nathaniel tucked it inside his jacket pocket. As he and John turned to leave, though, Nathaniel wanted to find out more about the rumors circulating throughout the colony.

"Dr. Warren, pardon me for being direct, but do you have any information regarding troop activity that we should bring back to our militia commander?"

The doctor was slightly surprised, but he took Nathaniel's arm and pulled him into a side room. "Yes, Nathaniel, something is going on. I have received notice that the officers have been discussing some type of action, but I don't have all the details. We've seen the activities of the grenadiers and light infantry change in the past couple of days. They were taken off their regular routines for some unknown reason. Once we know more here in the city, we will send couriers out to inform the countryside. Tell your Captain Parker to be on the alert."

"Yes, sir. Thank you for having confidence in us," Nathaniel replied.

"I know your family well enough to know you are not Loyalists. Be careful if something happens in the next few days. Are you doing anything else while in Boston?"

"We want to stop at Colonel Knox's bookstore, and I promised John that I would take him for dinner at the Green Dragon," Nathaniel said.

"Please say hello to Henry for me. Smart man. I've had many conversations with him based on his extensive reading and studying of military strategy. Green Dragon is a great place, but be careful. It is used by local patriots, Loyalists, and the military, so there will always be a mix of people with different—and sometimes volatile—opinions," Dr. Warren warned.

Before they left, Nathaniel said, "We missed speaking to your wife as we arrived. Please give her our best."

Dr. Warren's eyes opened wide, but he said, "My wife, Elizabeth, died young a couple of years ago. Let's keep that fine woman you saw between the three of us, all right?"

John and Nathaniel looked at each other and said at the same time, "Of course."

They carried their cloths and tools back to the wagon, climbed onto the bench seat, and gave the horses the command to move. When planning the trip into the city, Nathaniel had looked forward to getting to Henry Knox's bookstore to pick up some new reading material for the family, using some of the proceeds from the clock sale. They went back down Tremont Street, turned onto Queen Street, and proceeded to the Cornhill Street Alley, stopping outside the London Bookstore. Nathaniel had met the portly Mr. Knox on earlier trips into Boston and found the bookstore fascinating.

"Great idea," John said as they walked inside. "Mother's copy of *Pilgrim's Progress* is really worn."

CHAPTER 5

Mr. Knox greeted them as he did most customers—jovially and with a loud hello. Short and stocky, he was friendly with a great sense of humor. This made him well-liked throughout the city, but he was also highly respected for his military knowledge and expertise on certain weapons, especially cannons.

"Welcome, gentlemen," he said, rushing over to help Nathaniel and John.

"Good day, Mr. Knox. We are looking for a new copy of *Pilgrim's Progress* as well as some other reading material for family members. Any suggestions?" asked Nathaniel.

"Are you interested in anything in particular?"

John answered, "Something for our younger sister and brother."

Henry nodded and walked over to a large bookshelf inside the front window, pulling out two books and bringing them for the brothers to see. "Here are two good ones to choose from—adventure stories but with morality lessons, which is so important for young people. *Robinson Crusoe*, about a man stranded on an island after making some poor choices about his life. And *Gulliver's Travels*, the story of a man who visits many unusual lands and finds that common sense and compassion matter."

"We'll take both," said Nathaniel.

"I understand you have a wide selection of books on military subjects as well," John said. "Our brother, Sam, would really like something along that line."

"Ah, military is my specialty," said Henry. "I have a new volume on cannons I think he would enjoy." He reached under his counter and pulled up another book, adding it to their pile. "Tell him the middle section on proper positioning of cannons is very informative."

"One more thing, if you don't mind," added Nathaniel. "Do you have any old copies of *Poor Richard's Almanack*? Mary and Lydia would like those."

"Absolutely. Just give me a minute to get those in the back." He walked to the rear of the store and returned with two copies, as well as their original request for their mother. He put all the material in a canvas bag, handing the books to John while Nathaniel removed currency from the envelope from Dr. Warren.

"Thank you, Mr. Knox," Nathaniel said.

"My pleasure, indeed, young men. So glad to provide books for people who read and appreciate."

They left the store, climbed onto their wagon, and headed to Union Street for the Green Dragon tavern. It was easy to identify, with its large dragon sign hanging outside, the original copper turned green with age. They found a table with two chairs against a side wall and asked the tavernkeeper for some mead and two bowls of stew.

As they ate, a man walked behind them, obviously impaired from too much drinking. He bumped John as he passed, turning and staring at them.

"What, you aren't going to say 'excuse me?'" the man asked angrily.

"It was you who bumped into me, you clumsy fool," John replied without even looking up at him.

"So, you're looking for trouble, are you?" the man yelled, his face turning red and his eyes opening wide. "Well, you've found it here in Patrick Barnicle."

"Whoa, there," said Nathaniel, standing up to get between Patrick and John. "We don't want any trouble. Just enjoying a quick meal before heading back to Lexington."

"Lexington? I didn't think you were from around here. Haven't seen you here before. You farm boys here to help smuggle for Hancock, or are you part of the street rats run by Sam Adams?"

"No, sir, just had business in town with Dr. Warren," Nathaniel explained.

"Oh, part of the 'liberty' scum that meet downstairs? We Loyalists don't want you in here." Several other men had gathered behind him.

John stood up. "We just came to deliver a clock, you pea-brain blunderbuss. And your king is a tyrant. We would all be better off without him." Some other men walked over and stood behind John.

"This man is right, Barnicle," one said. "Your king is making it harder for all of us to make a living for our families."

Nathaniel could feel the heightened tension reaching a boiling point and decided they should probably leave. Fortunately, just at

CHAPTER 5

that moment, a group of uniformed soldiers entered the tavern, and everyone moved aside so they could get by.

"Come on, John, we have a long ride home," Nathaniel said, guiding his brother toward the exit.

"Hey, farm boy! Long live the king!" shouted Patrick.

John turned to reply, but Nathaniel pushed him out of the door, telling his brother, "John, there will be a time and a place to handle this, but not now and not here."

"I know, but he was looking for a fight."

Nathaniel patted him on the shoulder. "Another time, another place, my brother."

John nodded, and they climbed onto their wagon and headed out of Boston, anxious to leave a smoldering powder keg behind.

CHAPTER 6

April 18, 1775
Late afternoon

After checking on Isaac Walker and visiting with friend, Nathan Meriam, in town, Samuel prepared for his supper with the Mullikens. He was looking forward to seeing Lydia, and he also wanted to discuss the rising tensions in the colony with Nathaniel. Samuel's mother, Abigail, had made a nice raisin bread for him to bring to the Mullikens. He got Duchess ready, brushing her, securing his saddle, and feeding her a carrot from their root cellar before mounting her and heading toward Lexington late in the afternoon.

The ride from Concord, through Lincoln, and into Lexington was so routine for Duchess that Samuel didn't have to guide her; she just trotted along as if she knew exactly where they were going. It allowed Samuel time to daydream a little, reflecting back on how his relationship with his beloved had started.

A year before, Lydia's youngest brother, Joseph, had been in Concord for a church fair and had fallen out of a tree that he had been climbing with his friends on the town common. Some of the parish women started screaming for a doctor, and Samuel had been nearby, talking to Amos Melvin. When Samuel heard their cries, he rushed over to help. Joseph had only bruised his shoulder, but he had a hard time lifting his arm; Dr. Prescott gave him a ride home, which was how he met Lydia. He was immediately smitten by her beauty and kindness. They talked for a while, and he knew she was someone

CHAPTER 6

special. He asked if he could continue to visit with her regularly, and he had been so pleased when she agreed.

They had spent many weeks after that first meeting going to each other's Sunday services, Samuel meeting her in Lexington to hear Reverend Jonas Clarke's fiery orations or taking Lydia to hear Reverend Emerson at Concord's meetinghouse. There were many dinners shared at each other's homes, and both families enjoyed the future addition to their family. Still, his favorite memory was their first time truly alone one day during the previous June. His mind wandered back to that day...

Samuel picked Lydia up with his father's carriage, pulled by their largest horse, Atlas, a large white horse with a flowing white mane. They were going to have a quiet picnic in the meadows along the Concord River. Each of them commented on certain homes they passed along the way through Lincoln, knowing one family or another. After riding into Concord from Lexington, Samuel stopped the carriage at the edge of Reverend Emerson's fields, just up the lane from the North Bridge. He tied the horse to a low-hanging branch on a sturdy maple, lifted a wicker basket and quilt from behind the seat, and offered his hand to help Lydia step down.

She smiled at him as she took his hand, "Thank you, Samuel. You are such a gentleman."

As they started down the gravel lane toward the river, she put her right hand inside his left arm, just below the elbow, and they walked the hundred yards to the bridge. He could feel her fingers occasionally squeezing his arm as they walked. Across the river, a dozen deer paused to look at them and then bounded away. The river was flowing gently and quietly beneath the wooden bridge with its slight arch, nothing like months earlier when it had swelled over the banks from spring rains.

As they crossed the bridge, Samuel and Lydia stopped along the rails on the right side, watching several ducks gliding along the edge of the river and searching for food. The colorful males and brown females would pop up their tails and submerge their heads, finding morsels along the way. Upon reaching the other side, Samuel guided Lydia to a small slope facing the river in a meadow of daisies and wild lupine. He put down the quilt his mother had let him borrow about twenty feet from the river so they could sit quietly and comfortably even if the grass was damp.

From his wicker basket, he took out some fresh bread his sister, Lucy, had made for them, pulling apart several pieces. He then divided up a few pieces of roasted chicken, which they wrapped in the bread to eat. They also enjoyed some assorted fruit and pepper cakes—made of ground pepper, molasses, candied fruit and berries—and drank cider that Samuel poured from a silver flask into crystal glasses he had packed.

Samuel laid back, resting on his elbows and looking at the river. Lydia sat near him, slowly drinking her cider. He pointed out a hawk soaring above them and surveying the countryside in the greying sky. Watching as the calm river quietly flowed past them, Samuel suggested, "Sometime later this summer, we should borrow the reverend's boat and float down the river."

Lydia laughed. "But I don't know how to swim."

"Something I will have to teach you, maybe. My brothers and I have come here for years whenever summer gets too hot in town."

As they relaxed and shared family memories, Lydia noticed small splashes on the water, first randomly but soon appearing faster and stronger. It was starting to rain!

Samuel put whatever he could grab into the basket and rolled up the quilt. "Quick," he said, "get under that large elm over there." He pointed to a large tree several feet behind them. "The branches should provide us some shelter."

Lydia lifted her skirt and ran under the tree while Samuel wrapped the quilt around his arm and carried the basket. At first, the soft rain didn't reach them as the leaves of the elm protected them, but as it came down heavier, it began dripping on them. Samuel put down the basket, unfolded the quilt, and put it over them as they huddled together, his right hand holding one end and Lydia's left hand holding the other.

"I'm sorry, Lydia. I didn't expect it to rain today."

"I love adventures, Dr. Prescott," she replied, smiling up at him and gazing into his bright-blue eyes.

He looked deeply into her dark-brown eyes, seeing his reflection there. And then, for the first time, he kissed her. Briefly at first, but then longer and harder as she leaned into him. While his right hand held onto

CHAPTER 6

the quilt, his placed his left hand on the small of her back and pulled her closer.

The loud crack of musket fire snapped him out of his daydream as he reached Lexington Green. It was a triangular grassy area where the road from Boston split to either side, one road going to Bedford, the other—that he was on—going to Concord. To his left, he saw several militiamen just off the Green, firing their muskets, the grey smoke rising above them and hanging in the air. It was customary to unload weapons before entering a tavern, which they were doing before marching to Buckman Tavern next to the Green. Samuel continued past the center of town and approached the Mulliken house on the right.

When he arrived at Lydia's, Joseph ran out to greet him. As the youngest, he always enjoyed "company." He was thrilled when Samuel gave him the raisin bread and ran into the house, shouting, "Look what Dr. Prescott brought for me!"

They exchanged pleasantries but prepared to eat as everyone was hungry. Nathaniel and John had brought back two large cod from Salem that Mrs. Mulliken and Lydia had roasted. Mary had also made potatoes and root vegetables. Samuel smiled at Lydia as Rebeckah and Joseph kept asking him questions. He also noticed that Nathaniel was deep in thought and seemed more concerned than usual.

While Mrs. Mulliken, Lydia, and Mary cleared the table and stored the remaining food, Rebeckah and Joseph worked on their lessons in the *New England Primer* on the floor. Their brother, Sam, sat with them to help. Samuel joined Nathaniel and John who were in the main room, having a very animated discussion.

"Nathaniel and John, did you hear something in town regarding tensions in Boston or the countryside? You seem distracted and concerned," he asked.

Nathaniel answered, "When we dropped off the clock at Dr. Warren's yesterday, he told me about discussions regarding unusual troop activities. Dr. Warren knows the pulse of the city and can read the climate. He monitors all activities of the king's forces. He knows John and I are part of Captain Parker's group so didn't even try to dismiss it and actually asked me as we were leaving to tell Captain Parker to be on the alert."

Samuel looked around to see if they could be overheard and whispered quietly, "In Concord, there has been talk that Dr. Warren may have a relationship with General Gage's wife. Perhaps he is getting information through her?"

Nathaniel and John looked at each other.

"I bet that's the woman we saw leaving his house!" John shouted. He kept standing up, sitting down, then standing up again and pacing the floor.

"Nathaniel, we must do something!" he shouted.

"My dear brother, be patient. Captain Parker will signal if and when we are needed."

"Meanwhile, we sit here, doing nothing." John was exasperated.

"Well, what do you want us to do, John? Round everyone up and march on Boston? We will do what Captain Parker says when he gives us the orders. Now, calm down before we upset the rest of the family."

Samuel related to them the discussion at Wright's Tavern a few days before, including the transfer of supplies from the Barrett farm to Groton. He stressed the tensions described by John Masters. This only made John more uneasy.

"So, we just sit here and let them make the first move? Better to move needlessly than to be caught off guard. As Reverend Clarke suggested, we need to stand up for ourselves."

Nathaniel thought for a minute, then stood up, nodding his head.

"All right, my brother, let's go to Buckman Tavern and join the men gathered there. Perhaps we can calm you down by walking a bit in the night air. We can have Sam gather some supplies from the house and put them in the clock shop in case they are needed, without being too obvious. Do you want to join us, Dr. Prescott?"

"I appreciate the invitation, Nathaniel, but this is a Lexington decision. You will know what is best. Besides, I don't want to alarm Lydia."

CHAPTER 6

John and Nathaniel shook his hand as they made ready to leave. Nathaniel put on his coat and tricorn hat while John put on his round, wide-brimmed hat. Just as they walked to the door, Lydia came into the room.

"Sorry, Lydia, but we have some militia business to attend to." Nathaniel put his hands on her shoulders. "Spend some time with Dr. Prescott until we return."

He smiled at Samuel and left with John after giving their brother, Sam, his task of gathering supplies.

Lydia reached for her coat and said to Samuel, "Come, Mr. Prescott, let us take a walk too. But I have something to show you more interesting than militia talk."

Samuel put on his jacket and followed her out of the rear of the house.

They walked slowly, arm in arm, along the sandy path among the few tall pines in the area. The rain from earlier in the day had left some small puddles for them to avoid as they strolled toward the hill a short distance ahead. The scent of pine from a few broken branches lying on the path drifted on the soft April breeze. The spring sky was clearing, and the bright stars that occasionally appeared between the drifting clouds flickered softly.

"Did you enjoy your meal?" Lydia asked.

"Not as much as I enjoyed your company," Samuel replied.

She glanced up at him and smiled.

In the dark, the slope of the small hill seemed steeper. Samuel helped Lydia up the hill, holding her arm and occasionally putting his arm around her waist and guiding her. She led the way, as if she knew this area well.

"We're almost there," Lydia said with a hint of mischief in her voice.

Samuel noticed a large rock up ahead, flat on top and surrounded by a large, open area.

"Look!" she said, turning and pointing toward the center of the village. "You can see the light from the candles in the windows at Buckman Tavern. The meetinghouse on the Green is dark, but behind it, Jonathan and Ruth Harrington's rooms are bright and cheery."

Samuel answered, "This is spectacular, Lydia. No wonder you like to come here."

"But best of all," she continued, "look above us. So many stars, such a beautiful sky!"

As if on cue, the clouds had parted, and the sky was clearer.

Lydia went on, speaking with awe and wonder in her voice. "Tonight it is clearer than the last time I came. There are so many shapes and pictures you can find in the stars. I love to come here, sit on the rock, and imagine all the other people in the world who are looking up at the same sky."

Samuel laid back on the top of the rock and gazed into the night sky. It was quiet and peaceful here. Up above, the twinkling of the brightest stars seemed so comforting. He said to Lydia, "I'll have to do this from our fields some night and think of you up here, looking at the same stars."

She laughed then leaned over and kissed him. For the first time that night, Samuel noticed a purple ribbon tying up the back of her hair.

"That ribbon looks very nice and has such a sweet fragrance. What is it?" he asked.

"It is lavender. Remember the beautiful plants in my mother's garden last year? She crushes the lavender flowers and dyes ribbons for us, giving them color and a long-lasting fragrance."

"I hope Nathaniel's concerns don't affect that garden this summer," Samuel said, sitting up and suddenly appearing worried. "If what he says about the Regulars is true, we could have a very disturbing summer in this colony."

"Nathaniel sometimes worries *too* much, Samuel. We'll be too busy planning our own lives and the wedding."

"That's what concerns me. Why do we have to wait until next year to be married? Let's have the wedding sooner. I don't want anything to interfere with us being together."

CHAPTER 6

Lydia placed her right hand gently on Samuel's left cheek. Gazing into his troubled eyes, she spoke softly, trying to reassure and comfort him.

"In ordinary times, we would be able to set the wedding date and plan toward it without worries. I would like nothing more than to spend the next weeks and months thinking only of the day we pledge to spend our lives together. But these are not ordinary times, and despite our extraordinary love for each other, we both know there are so many things to be concerned with now. These troubled times will pass, but my love for you will always be here, waiting patiently. Nothing, *absolutely nothing*, will change that. Changing seasons, life's challenges, even these threats of rebellion cannot stop me from becoming your wife. You are now, and will always be, the love of my life."

The hoofbeats of several horses passing on the road below caught their attention.

"We must go back," Lydia said with disappointment in her voice. The occasional crack of a musket firing in the distance added urgency to their steps.

As they returned to the Mulliken house, they saw more activity than would be expected around midnight on a spring Tuesday. In the brightly lit main room, Nathaniel and John were sitting with one of their lifelong friends, Caleb Harrington, who Lydia recognized as a member of the town "training band" or militia. She introduced him to Samuel. At that moment, Nathaniel jumped to his feet.

"Samuel, you should make your way home immediately. We have received scouting reports that the Regulars may be approaching on their way to Concord."

This was a moment Lydia had feared after their evening discussions. She had accepted the fact that her brothers would participate in any action taken in town but did not want her young love to be in danger.

"Quickly, my darling, be on your way," she said, some urgency reflected in the tone of her voice.

Samuel could also sense the fear in her voice and looked steadily into her eyes.

"Don't worry, Lydia. I'll be home in no time, as the road from here to Concord should be quiet." He reached out and gently placed his fingertips under her chin. "Be calm, my love, I will be fine," he said, trying to reassure her. "I shall come by tomorrow evening, and we will all talk some more about our futures."

Lydia threw her arms around his neck and held him tightly. "I will count the seconds until you come back to me, though they will seem like years. I love you, Samuel."

Samuel kissed her on her forehead. "And I love you, Lydia. Sleep well, and we'll be together again before you know it."

Then he turned to leave.

"Wait, Samuel!" Lydia untied the purple ribbon from her hair and placed it softly in his hand. Her hands folded his fingers around the ribbon. "Take this for luck."

Samuel smiled then nodded farewell to the men. In an instant, he stepped out the door, mounted his horse, and was gone.

Lydia stared at the closed door. Her body ached, wanting to run through it and hold him back.

Chapter 7

April 18, 1775
Nightfall

Major Pitcairn readied his horse at the Boston army stables, checking his saddlebag to be sure his pistols were packed and secured properly. He mounted his horse and headed across to the Boston Common rendezvous site before nine o'clock. He wanted to help organize the transfer of troops to Phipps Farm in East Cambridge as they were loaded and unloaded from the longboats which would transport them across the harbor. As requested by General Gage, Pitcairn was assisting in the mission to help Colonel Smith even though his own Marines were not participating.

The plan was to have the troops assembled by ten o'clock and in formation to march shortly after midnight, giving them plenty of time for a surprise arrival in Concord by dawn. However, when Pitcairn arrived at the rendezvous spot, he was stunned to find very few men ready for a ten o'clock assembly. He found one of the junior officers nearby and requested information.

"Lieutenant! What has happened? Why aren't there more troops prepared for the march?" Pitcairn asked, agitated that they weren't ready.

"Major, we had some problems, as a couple of the officers overslept and didn't wake their troops on time," answered the young man.

"Have you seen Colonel Smith?" replied Major Pitcairn, looking around, concerned that even the commanding officer was not present.

"He hasn't arrived yet, sir," said the officer, shaking his head.

At that moment, a sergeant walked up to Major Pitcairn, pointing at the steeple of the Old North Church, visible from the troop staging area. "Major, you have been in Boston as long as I have. Have you ever seen that steeple lighted?" he asked.

As Pitcairn turned to look, the steeple once again went black. "No, Mackenzie, but it looks like it is out now. Let's get the troops moving."

But the two lanterns in the steeple already had their intended effect—riders, including Paul Revere and William Dawes, were on their way, spreading the alarm.

Major Pitcairn turned and rode back to the area where the men were gathering along the shore. He asked one of the naval officers who was there to start loading the men present into the longboats. There were about twenty boats, requiring two trips each to carry all the planned forces across the Charles River. When they were unloaded on the other shore at Lechmere Point, the troops collected in an area that was partially marshland. As time went by, the incoming tide started rising, and many of the men were in water up to their knees. The major moved them further inland while he continued to search for Colonel Smith. The troops were given thirty-six rounds of ammunition and a day's rations of food. Smith arrived shortly after and told Pitcairn that he thought the men were supposed to depart the barracks at ten then assemble for midnight.

It was now almost two o'clock in the morning.

"Regardless, Colonel," snapped Major Pitcairn. "We are starting late. I have the advance guards ready to move. Shall I get them started?"

"Yes, Major. Proceed. You may lead the way, and I will remain further back to command the remaining light infantry and grenadiers. Let me know of any concerns as you march forward."

Pitcairn turned his horse and said to Smith, "There is a wooden bridge up ahead as we leave Phipps Farm. I suggest we have the men wade through the shallow creek rather than cross the bridge. The sound of men crossing the bridge could alert someone that we are marching."

CHAPTER 7

"As you wish, Major."

The major saluted, turned his horse, and galloped to the front of the formation. He ordered two of the younger officers to lead the way and rode alongside as the formation started on their way west, almost four hours later than had been planned. As he sat on his horse and watched the men wade through the creek, he was approached by one of the junior officers.

"Major, some of the men are wondering what this foray into the countryside is all about," the officer asked.

"In due time, Ensign, in due time," replied Pitcairn. "Colonel Smith has specific orders directly from General Gage and will share them with the troops at the appropriate time. In the meantime, tell your men to maintain their pace."

The ensign turned and joined the lead groups entering the road toward Lexington and Concord.

Less than an hour after the start of the mission, the advance group encountered a rider who appeared to be some type of scout. "Stop!" shouted one of the junior officers. "Where are you going, and what is the purpose of your trip?"

The man looked back and forth at the officers and the many soldiers standing in front of him. His hesitation to answer irritated Pitcairn. "At this time of the night, if you don't know where you are going, it must be improper. Take him and his horse, Lieutenant."

The man was apprehended, his horse taken away, and he was sent to the rear of the formation to be held. The Regulars came across several more riders who were also seized as the mission moved through Menotomy (now Arlington), the town just east of Lexington. The soldiers began hearing occasional musket fire as well as an occasional church bell, leaving them to suspect that alarms were being sent and their "surprise" mission was clearly no surprise at all. One of the scouts they stopped and seized told them there were a thousand militia waiting for them in Lexington. Major Pitcairn had one junior officer ride back to tell Colonel Smith, who dispatched an aide to Boston, requesting reinforcements. Pitcairn was not happy with the new circumstances and ordered the men to pick up the pace of their march.

Chapter 8

April 19, 1775
After midnight

The return trip from Lexington always seemed longer. He hated leaving Lydia and longed for the day when it wouldn't be necessary. As he passed the dark and quiet Lexington Green, a place that would see pain and horror in a few hours, Samuel reached into his coat pocket and removed the ribbon Lydia had given him. While it circled his hand, entwined in his fingers, he held it to his nose. The sweet lavender fragrance was still there, bringing a smile to his face.

The almost calm April breeze carried the scent of smoke still rising from smoldering fireplaces along his way. As the night cooled, there was a damp mist hanging over the packed gravel road. Entering the road that turned toward Lincoln, the young doctor overtook two riders ahead of him. They were speaking with urgency and firmness, gesturing toward the houses that were spread thinly along the road in front of them. Samuel put Lydia's ribbon back into his pocket, and as he approached, one of the riders turned to him.

"Pleasant evening, sir. Bit late to be out, isn't it?" the man asked. He seemed suspicious that someone would be riding at that time of night on such a quiet country road.

Samuel replied, "Just returning from an enjoyable meal and some wonderful company in Lexington. Are you gentlemen lost?"

"No, quite the contrary. I've traveled this path often delivering news to local towns. My name is Revere, Paul Revere."

CHAPTER 8

"And I am William Dawes, my friend," said the other man as he rode up next to Samuel.

"Pleased to make your acquaintance, gentlemen. I'm Doctor Samuel Prescott of Concord. Can I offer any assistance?"

Mr. Revere responded, careful what he wanted to reveal about their mission. "Actually, we were intending to continue to Concord, alerting the inhabitants along the way to some news from Boston of a serious nature."

"Are you referring to military action? If you are alerting people that the Regulars are out, allow me to join you!" Samuel exclaimed. "I know this area and its people well and want to help."

Dawes and Revere seemed somewhat surprised that Samuel was aware of the situation but were pleased.

"We are glad you appear to be a Son of Liberty." Dawes smiled. "How did you know about the troops?"

"My friends in Lexington have been busy most of the night gathering reports. They are preparing to protect their town as we speak."

Revere nodded. "I am a simple silversmith in Boston but have been asked many times to be a courier for Doctor Warren and the colonial leaders in the city. I was told the Regulars were indeed preparing to leave Boston, proceeding toward Concord, looking for weapons and supplies. Mr. Dawes and I met at Reverend Clarke's house in Lexington to warn Samuel Adams and John Hancock of the activity. At first, Mr. Hancock wanted to grab a musket and muster with the militia, but Mr. Adams reminded him they weren't soldiers. Mr. Adams was thrilled with the news as he has been waiting for something to trigger some type of action in the colony. You are welcome to join us."

"Well, gentlemen, if the Regulars are indeed marching toward my town, I insist. We must alert as many homes along the way as we can."

Revere agreed. "If we split up, we can each take a house as we pass, moving along more rapidly. Timing is a serious problem. It is urgent we get the message out before the Regulars get close. The alarm needs to be given to as many towns as possible before they can destroy any supplies."

Prescott suggested, "My family and I have cared for many of these people. Our warning will surely be more well received if I accompany either of you to the door."

"Splendid," said Revere. "Do not spend time discussing what is happening. Just tell them we are spreading the alarm so they will be ready. But be alert. I escaped a patrol earlier tonight leaving Boston, and I'm sure there are many others out on the road tonight. The patrols will be angry if they know we are spreading the news. The troops want and need some measure of surprise for their mission to be successful, which is why they started as this time of the night."

The men took turns riding up to each house, first Prescott and Dawes while Revere went to the next, and then Prescott and Revere while Dawes went ahead. At each house, one of them would pound on the door, apologize for the disturbance or for startling them, and notify the homeowner of the impending threat. The houses were usually right along the road, some in clusters, others spread out more thinly. They were colonial farmhouses with doors in the center, windows on either side of the door, and a row of three to five windows on the upper floor; a few of the homes were saltboxes with long, sloping roofs in the rear, many with some type of outer building or barn. Most had a center fireplace. As Samuel and Dawes approached one of the houses on the Lexington/Lincoln line, Samuel recognized it as one that he knew well, the home of Nathaniel Baker, a Lincoln minuteman.

"Nathaniel! Nathaniel Baker!" Samuel shouted as he pounded on the side of the house.

A young man came out of the front door, accompanied by a young lady.

"Samuel Prescott, what are you doing out at this hour?" the man asked.

"Just returning from visiting Lydia, but have some urgent news for you. The Regulars are out and marching on Concord."

"I was having a late dinner with my fiancée, Elizabeth," Nathaniel said, pointing at the young lady. He turned to her, saying,

CHAPTER 8

"I must go, my dear. I have to notify our militia leader." He thanked Samuel, mounted a horse tied to the fence in back, and hurried off as Elizabeth returned to the house. Samuel and Dawes turned up the road.

Samuel gave Duchess a pat on the neck as he and Dawes approached another house. She had had a long day, having left her stable in the afternoon and traveling quite a distance. He removed an apple he had stored in his saddle bag for her, and she shook her head with approval as he placed it in her mouth. He looked up and he saw Revere on the roadway several hundred feet ahead of them. Suddenly two British officers, easily identified by their red jackets and white knickers, charged out from under some trees.

"Watch out!" warned Revere.

Prescott and Dawes rushed up to meet him and help fight off the officers, Samuel turning his whip to use it as a weapon if necessary. Just then, another group of riders, also in uniform, came at them from the other side of the road, surrounding him and Revere. As Dawes was slightly behind them, he turned quickly and escaped by riding in the other direction, confusing the patrol by yelling, "I've got them!"

The officers in the patrol pointed their pistols at Prescott and Revere, directing the two riders into a pasture just off the road. The rails of a fence had been removed, and the patrol guided them into the field. Samuel sensed a tension and agitation among the officers. Looking around, he knew there was an old farm road off to the left that passed through dense brush and a swampy area; it was an area he had traveled many times over the years when he tried to find shorter distances between the homes of patients he would visit.

He tightened the grip on his reins, looked over at Revere, and whispered, "Put on!" As he spoke, he dug his heels into Duchess and turned her head hard left.

She responded as Samuel knew she would. With a burst of speed, she leapt over a stone wall, dashed between several large trees, and onto the overgrown, abandoned dirt path. Glancing quickly over his right shoulder, Samuel saw some of the officers had chased and captured Revere. Two others were in pursuit of him.

He remembered from his past trips that there was a wet, muddy section of the path slightly ahead, with sagging, old grapevines on the right side and a narrow, raised, more-solid area to the left. He guided his horse to that side of the path.

"Stop!" yelled one of the pursuers. As Samuel had planned, this rider went straight into the soft, wet clay in the center of the path, stopping his horse in its tracks. The other rider swerved to the right to miss the spot but became tangled in the hanging vines and fell off his horse.

Once he was sure he was no longer being pursued, Samuel turned left, through the woods, and back toward the main road. He wasn't sure how far he was from town, but he let Duchess find her way through the trees and fields, avoiding any other wet areas.

Up ahead, he saw the dark silhouette of a house. Breaking through some tangled brush, he rode into the backyard. There was a candle burning in one room downstairs, sending a dim light into the night air. Cautiously, he rode up to the back door, dismounted, and knocked twice.

"Who is it at this hour?" he heard a woman say through the closed door.

"Sorry to disturb you, madam, but I am spreading an alarm. The Regulars have left Boston and are headed this way on their way to Concord. The word must be sent out."

He listened carefully and heard the door being unlatched. When it opened, a woman stood there, holding a very young infant.

"And who are you?" she asked, looking at him as though she wasn't sure she should believe him.

"Dr. Samuel Prescott of Concord," he replied. "I am returning home from Lexington, trying to inform as many homes as possible. I'm sorry if I disturbed you or your child."

"Not a problem, young man. It was feeding time, and I was up anyways. This is the home of Sergeant Samuel Hartwell, so I am accustomed to late night visits. I am his wife, Mary. News of the Regulars on the march is important. Please come in."

"Thank you, but I must continue on my way. There are many more stops before I get to the center of town."

CHAPTER 8

Just then, a young servant girl from the West Indies, disheveled and half awake, stumbled into the room. "Miss Mary, what is going on?" she asked, yawning and rubbing her eyes.

"Sukey, we need your help. Could you please run down to Captain Smith's house and let him know the Regulars are marching on Concord?"

Sukey gasped. "Oh, no. Please don't ask me to do that. If they catch me out there, they will capture me. Or there may be wild animals out tonight. Please, Miss Mary, please." She started crying.

The woman looked at Samuel then back at Sukey. Mary bundled up her baby, carefully holding the infant out toward the girl.

"Here, Sukey, take my child. I will go. Captain Smith will probably respond faster if he hears details from me anyways. Let my husband know, and I will be right back."

As she ran out of the house, Samuel followed her and climbed onto Duchess. Sukey called out to Sergeant Hartwell to wake him with the news.

"Thank you, and good luck!" Samuel heard Mary say as she headed toward the next farm, which was just a short distance away.

Samuel spurred Duchess out around the house and back onto the road to Concord. Next door was the Hartwell Tavern. Samuel pounded on the front door and then a front window, shouting, "The Regulars are out, marching to Concord." He stopped at the windows of several other homes as he passed and yelled out the alarm. Sometimes he pounded on doors; at others he yelled through a window. At most houses, candles or lanterns would be lit as he rode away.

Before leaving Lincoln, Samuel alarmed a cluster of homes owned by the Brooks family then continued past Nathan and Abigail Meriam's house as he came into Concord. Approaching Concord center and passing by his own house, he stopped at Amos Melvin's house. Samuel knew Amos had duty this week to sound the town meetinghouse alarms.

"Amos, the alarm bell must be rung so the townspeople will know of the alert," he told him when Amos came to the door.

"Samuel, what news have you heard?'

"The Regulars have already left Boston and are heading in this direction, looking to destroy any of the weapons and supplies stored here. We need to get everyone ready."

"I am on my way, Samuel." Amos ran out of his door and headed to the meetinghouse.

Samuel visited a few other homes nearby, including Dr. Timothy Minot's, another doctor in town, to pass the word. Then he heard the loud ringing of the town meetinghouse bell. As he rode out of the center of town, heading back home, he noticed Reverend Emerson coming into town with his musket, the first to respond to the alarm. The reverend joined three companies of minutemen assembling at Wright's Tavern, awaiting orders from their commander, Captain John Buttrick. Amos and David Suttle went to Colonel Barrett's farm to help hide any remaining barrels of musket balls and flints, moving many into the attic and covering them with feathers or manure in the barn. Some additional muskets that had not been moved were buried in furrows already dug in the field, covered before the farm could be inspected by the Regulars who would be sent there later that morning.

At home, he found everyone awake from the sounding of the alarm. He hurriedly put Duchess into the barn and ran inside. His father and older brothers, Benjamin and Abel, were discussing their next moves, with the elder doctor suggesting Abel ride farther north or south to notify other towns after hearing the alarm bell. Abel turned as Samuel rushed into the room, noticing the mud splattered on his boots and trousers.

"Well, little brother, it looks as though your night was rather interesting. What do you know?"

"Apparently, the Regulars have already left Boston and are heading here, looking for weapons and supplies. Lydia's brothers received the news and are with the Lexington militia as we speak. I can head back out, going west to spread the alarm."

His father spoke. "I am pleased at your involvement, Samuel. But you look tired. Abel can continue spreading the alarm."

Samuel smiled. "I'm tired, Father, but I can rest tomorrow. There is work to be done—freedom's duty calls. I have been so absorbed

CHAPTER 8

with caring for patients I didn't put as much stock in the impending dangers, but what we have heard in town recently and my discussions with Lydia's brothers have me committed to help now. But Duchess cannot go on at this point. Can I take one of the other horses?"

Abel grabbed his brother's arm as he pulled him toward the door. "Take whichever horse you want. Atlas has been resting all day, and Rascal was only out for a short time this evening. I will take Dusty. Benjamin can get Duchess settled for the night."

Benjamin followed them outside, brushed Duchess, rinsed the mud and dirt from her legs, and covered her with a warm blanket. Samuel and Abel quickly saddled up, and Abel headed south toward Sudbury and Framingham.

As they set out, Samuel yelled to his brother, "Be careful, Abel. There might be patrols out there. I encountered one on my way home."

Abel yelled back, "Thanks. I'll keep an eye open for them. You be careful too, and I'll see you at home sometime in the morning."

Samuel took Rascal, a bigger and stronger horse than Duchess, and headed back up Lexington Road toward town, passing several militiamen on the way. Rascal seemed to sense his urgency and was very responsive, quickly picking up speed. They turned left onto Main Street and headed west to spread the word to Acton, Maynard, and Stow. Approaching the Acton line, Samuel turned left onto Concord Road, knowing Captain Joseph Robbins, the Acton commander and a family friend, had a farm only a short distance away.

At the Robbins farm, he pounded on the outer wall of the house, yelling, "Captain Robbins, the Regulars are marching on Concord. Send the alarm."

Captain Robbins acknowledged the warning by calling out to his son. "John, take the horse and go to the Davis farm. Let Captain Davis know the Regulars are on their way to Concord. He will know what to do."

Young John, on his thirteenth birthday, rushed to let Captain Isaac Davis know about the alarm. Captain Davis thanked young John, grabbed his musket, and headed toward the center of Acton to join his men.

As the captain reached the edge of his property, he paused for a minute then turned and shouted back to his wife Hannah, "Take care of the children." He didn't know when he would be able to return home.

Leaving the Robbins farm, Samuel continued down the road through Acton into Maynard, alerting many of the houses along the way. He wanted to get to Stow before daylight. The cool, crisp air was invigorating, and the extreme importance of his mission had his adrenaline flowing. He reached into the pocket where he had put Lydia's ribbon and touched it briefly. Oh, he had such a story to tell her!

Meanwhile, as the Regulars entered Lexington, the patrol that had captured Revere and Prescott met up with the marching forces, and they told Major Pitcairn what they had encountered and forces were seen gathering in Lexington center. Concerned, Major Pitcairn stopped the lines of infantry and gave them the order to load their weapons and fix bayonets. The troops quickly prepared their muskets and put them back on their shoulders for the march. Some of them were grumbling about their feet being wet and the slow pace of the march; they were also alarmed at the news that they might be confronted by a large force ahead. Occasionally, they could see figures moving in the shadows deep in the darkness beside them. They were just passing Munroe Tavern, with the Mulliken house up ahead on their left and the Green almost within sight.

Inside the Mulliken house, Lydia and Mary sat quietly at the windows, which had been shuttered after Nathaniel and John left while the two youngest slept peacefully upstairs. The sisters heard the approaching soldiers and listened intently as they passed, the steady footsteps just feet from their windows. The shadows of the men passing could be seen through the small cracks in the shutters. Sam was next door in the clock shop with their mother, gathering some more supplies in the event they had to leave suddenly as Nathaniel and John had instructed. They stopped working to see the troops passing, on their way to meet the men of Lexington who were waiting for them.

PART 2

But if they mean to have a war let it begin here!

—Captain John Parker

Chapter 9

April 19, 1775
Early morning

After Samuel left, heading back to Concord, Nathaniel, John, and their friend, Caleb, rushed into the center of town, meeting some other militiamen at Buckman Tavern to see what additional news had been received. Buckman Tavern was located just to the side of the Green, along the road that turned toward Bedford, with stables in the back. Several of the men were getting impatient. Many of them sat in the taproom in front while others overflowed into the hallways. They had assembled at the sound of the ringing of the town belfry, knowing from earlier discussions that something serious was unfolding. Most were uneasy to be facing the king's army but also resolute in their need to do so. The tension and concern had many of them whispering to each other what they had heard.

"Are you sure they are really coming today, Captain?" Jebediah Munroe asked Captain Parker.

"A courier passed through town earlier, alerting many along the way of the Regulars leaving Boston. He also went to Reverend Clarke's home to warn John Hancock and Samuel Adams, since they may also be targets of the march. The courier then proceeded to Concord to warn them that destroying the supplies hidden there are an important part of the mission. Be patient."

"Maybe they got lost in the dark," Jonathan Harrington suggested from the hallway, causing some laughter.

CHAPTER 9

"They will be here soon enough," Captain Parker warned. "You can all wait here or go home and listen for either the belfry to ring the alarm or drummer, William Diamond, to send the drumbeat."

Nathaniel stayed but gave some instructions to John. "Go home. Let Mother, Mary, and Lydia know what has happened. Help Sam prepare the wagon with some supplies. Tell them to be ready to leave with whatever they can take to get through the day and maybe for tonight. Try not to alarm them, as I'm sure they will be concerned. Then come back, and we can wait together."

John ran back to the house, meeting Lydia at the front door.

"John, are you all right? Where is Nathaniel?" she asked.

"I'm fine. Nathaniel is waiting with our men. I'll go back to help him as soon as we can get you prepared to leave."

"Where do we go now?" his mother asked as she joined them in the doorway.

"Nathaniel sent me to tell you to gather some supplies and have Sam take you to a safe place in Woburn that we had planned for you. I'll tell Sam how to find it and help him get what you need. Plan on staying there until tomorrow morning, when we'll let you know it's safe to return. We're concerned that it will be even more dangerous after the Regulars pass through town and later have to make their way back to Boston when they are finished in Concord."

"When will we see you again, John?" Mary asked.

"I can't say, Mary," John replied. "Please take care of each other until we can get you home again safely tomorrow."

John helped Sam load the wagon that they used for clock deliveries with some blankets and supplies. For added protection, he made sure Sam was armed with one of the fowling guns they had stored in the clock shop. Together, they hid some valuable items in the clock shop while Lydia and Mary took some silver and other items and hid them in a stone wall behind the house as a precaution in case houses were looted by the army on its return march. Everyone tried to stay calm and focus on what needed to be done. As John was loading the last items into the wagon, he heard the drumbeat warning he had been waiting for, as well as the belfry bell; he hugged his mother and rushed back to the center of town, telling his mother as he left, "I'll let you know what happens and what to do next."

When John returned to Buckman Tavern, Nathaniel told him a scout had just reported to Captain Parker that he had seen the troops on the outskirts of town. They heard Captain Parker shout orders to his men. "Gather on the Green, but do not interfere with the troops or block their passage to Concord. Unless we are assaulted, let them pass. Stay in formation, waiting for further orders."

As the men left the tavern, Nathaniel stopped and looked at the tall clock in the corner of Buckman's taproom—one that had been made by his father. It was just after five o'clock.

Nathaniel and John joined the other men as they crossed from Buckman Tavern to the town Green, Nathaniel on one end, John and Caleb on the other. Caleb's father, Moses, at sixty-five, the oldest man there, stood with them. Behind them were Samuel Hadley, John Brown, and John Munroe. Caleb's cousin, Jonathan Harrington, was closer to Nathaniel but in a second line. Another man, Prince Estabrook, and an older man, Jebediah Munroe, were also in that group, standing near John Muzzy and his son, Isaac. Robert Munroe stood a few feet from Nathaniel.

There were about seventy of them: farmers, shopkeepers, tradesmen, some veterans of earlier wars; fathers, sons and brothers; uncles, nephews, and cousins. From sixteen to sixty-five, gathered together to defend their families and their property. And they were about to face an oncoming force of seven hundred of the mightiest military of the time.

Nathaniel felt his stomach tighten and his anxiety level rising. For the first time in his life, he was about to lift his gun and aim it at another man. Some doubt crept into his mind as he wondered to himself if he could actually *shoot* another person. He considered walking away, but his sense of duty steadied him. All the recent talk and ranting about the British tyranny and the hatred for the Regulars was intense, but to actually fire a weapon with the intent to kill was foreign to him. Sure, he had been hunting with his late father and his brothers since he was very young, but shooting a turkey, a rabbit, or a deer was different than looking down the barrel of your musket at

CHAPTER 9

a human being—especially a soldier from the feared king's army. He remembered how his father had told him the accuracy of a musket drops after about seventy yards; he had practiced enough to be fairly accurate at 100 yards, but hoped it wouldn't be necessary.

He swallowed hard as he looked across and saw John at the other end of the line. Captain Parker was issuing orders as he walked across in front of the lines of men, but Nathaniel felt as if he was in a thick morning fog, only partially hearing the captain's commands. He reached into his cartridge box. It held about twenty rounds of cartridges, made up of musket balls packed in gunpowder in paper packets. Carefully, he pulled back the hammer on his flintlock, tore open a packet with his teeth, then with his hand trembling as never before, poured some powder into the frizzen pan. He carefully closed the cover and poured the remaining powder with the musket ball into the barrel. Nathaniel slid the ramrod down the throat of his musket, packing the load into place. He looked at some of the older men in the group who still used powder horns, and they were pouring it into their muskets. He looked around the edges of the Green where several dozen spectators had gathered despite the early hour.

His hands were sweating, and despite the cool morning air, Nathaniel could feel the perspiration on his forehead and upper lip. He looked around him, gazing at the other men. Some seemed as tense as he was while others—like Jonas Parker—seemed to be enjoying the moment. There was little discussion between the men, but those who had been veterans of previous wars appeared much more comfortable. Nathaniel heard Caleb and two other men tell Captain Parker they needed more ammunition; the captain gave them permission to run into the meetinghouse on the front of the Green. Captain Parker also asked John to help two men, a Mr. Lowell and a Mr. Revere, remove a trunk of important papers that belonged to Mr. Hancock from Buckman Tavern, so John hurried across the road to assist.

Then Nathaniel heard it—a rhythmic stomping coming from the direction of his own house. Thousands of feet, slowly, steadily moving toward the Green and those waiting with him. Moments later, they could see the occasional flash of the early morning light reflected off bayonets. The bright red-and-white uniforms, contrasting with the black hats, started to come into full view.

Captain Parker shouted to his small band of men, "Stand your ground. Don't fire unless fired upon. But if they mean to have a war, let it begin here."

John returned to the edge of the Green, and two men carried a large trunk across the road, through the Green and past the lines of militia. They disappeared behind the houses beyond the Green.

Nathaniel swallowed hard. He understood what this moment meant to the safety and perhaps the future freedoms for his mother and his siblings. He knew and accepted his duty to them and Lexington. His anger toward the king's forces was again rising inside him. Still, he was scared. His grip on his musket continued to tighten as he held it, ready for use. Nathaniel knew he had to wait for orders from Captain Parker and do as was ordered, but he wasn't sure if he could even move. Once again, he glanced over at his brother, who suddenly seemed older to him. For the first time, John looked like a man rather than the irresponsible boy Nathaniel was accustomed to seeing.

Closer and closer, the mass of red uniforms approached. Many were hidden from view by the meetinghouse. A large group of redcoats came running around the left side of the meetinghouse, yelling, with their bayonets facing the Lexington men. Several officers on horseback came around to the right of the building while the group of foot soldiers advanced around to the left then stopped partway onto the Green.

One of those officers was Major Pitcairn. He raised one of his silver pistols over his head, yelling at the men gathered in front of him, "Disperse, you damn rebels. Lay down your arms. Go home!"

He looked directly into Nathaniel's eyes momentarily—a fateful encounter between two men with much different backgrounds and lifestyles, from different worlds, each there to defend his own. Then, turning away from Nathaniel, Pitcairn trotted his horse back and forth in front of the minutemen, continuing to demand that they drop their weapons and leave.

CHAPTER 9

Pitcairn shouted orders to the Regulars nearest to the minutemen, telling them, "Do not fire. Surround them and disarm them."

Nathaniel's heart was pounding so loud he could no longer hear the officer. Captain Parker was yelling something about dispersing, and some of the men next to and behind Nathaniel began moving. He looked over at John and saw him leave the Green, heading back toward Buckman Tavern. He was followed by Samuel Hadley and John Brown. Slowly Nathaniel turned to his left and started toward the back of the Green on a line to Jonathan Harrington's house, glancing back at the redcoats lining up across from him.

Suddenly the quiet of the morning was shattered by a volley of musket fire from the soldiers who had advanced around the left of the meetinghouse. A musket ball whistled past Nathaniel's right ear. He heard Jonathan Harrington yell out as another musket ball ripped into his chest just feet from Nathaniel. Another ball tore a hole in Nathaniel's coat, just under his left arm. He felt a sudden rush of terror and fear. Jonas Parker fell to the ground where he had been standing and was trying to raise his musket to return fire. Isaac Muzzy died at his father's feet. More shots rang out. There were men from both sides, running and shouting, with musket fire and the cries of the wounded minutemen filling the morning air. Screams from the bystanders added to the chaos and confusion. Nathaniel saw two of the three men who had gone into the meetinghouse for ammunition come out the door and try to escape by running toward the side of the Green; one was shot in the arm but kept going. Caleb Harrington, a lifelong friend, was shot in the back and fell to the ground. Nathaniel's heart skipped, as he felt pain for his friend. The soldiers continued to shout as they began running forward with their deadly bayonets pointed in his direction. Robert Munroe died just feet from where Nathaniel had been standing.

Looking over his shoulder as he continued toward the rear of the Green, Nathaniel saw John Munroe fire back, but his musket barrel exploded with wood and metal fragments flying everywhere; he had overloaded it. As old Jonas Parker struggled to get back up and raise his musket, one of the redcoats drove his bayonet through him, plunging the cold steel blade deep into his chest. Two of the men leaving the Green behind John Mulliken, Samuel Hadley and John Brown, were shot and killed as they crossed over to Buckman's. Another man, Asahel Porter from Woburn, who was among the men taken as prisoners earlier that morning, saw the Regulars distracted by events on the Green; he decided to try to escape, but was shot and killed.

Heavy smoke and the pungent smell of gunpowder filled the air over the Green. Jonathan Harrington, hurt badly, was desperately trying to crawl to his house at the rear of the Green. As Nathaniel left the Green, he saw Ruth, Jonathan's young wife, waiting for her husband on the stairs. Their ten-year-old son was watching, stunned and horrified, from an upstairs window.

Nathaniel crossed over the road at the edge of the Green and ran between the Harrington's house and a neighbor's house, almost to the edge of the Old Burial Grounds. Glancing behind him, he saw the soldiers were still pursuing members of the militia, stopping occasionally to fire at them. The officer who had looked at him was slashing his sword up and down, desperately trying to get the Regulars to stop firing and get back into formation. A drummer was beating the order to fall into formation. Within a few minutes, the pursuit stopped, and the soldiers were brought back into file by commands from the officers and the drummer. As Nathaniel stopped, panting from fear as much as from fatigue, he heard them yell three cheers. He was horrified that here on his town Green, with friends and neighbors dying in front of him, these killers were actually cheering. The reasons for the anger and fear that had been growing within town and among his associates was being displayed before him. His immediate concern, besides finding safety, was looking for John.

As the Regulars finished falling into order, their officers gathered at the edge of the Green.

Colonel Smith had come up as part of the rear of the long line of grenadiers. "What happened here?" he asked the officers.

Major Pitcairn spoke up. "Some of the men thought they heard a musket fired and opened fire themselves. Some of them lost control, but we were able to bring them back into formation."

"Any injuries to report?" asked Smith.

CHAPTER 9

One of the ensigns spoke up. "One man had a very minor leg wound but is fine."

Pitcairn said, "My horse was hit but has no damage."

Smith met with the officers and told them, for the first time, that their orders were to march to Concord to find and destroy any weapons or supplies. After what had just happened, some of the junior officers questioned the reasoning of continuing, but Colonel Smith reminded them that these were the orders directly from General Gage. Major Pitcairn agreed, and the officers gave commands for the entire group to begin marching along the road that went to Lincoln and Concord.

As the troops began their march along the edge of the Green, the bystanders who had watched in terror rushed to help those shot. Nathaniel went around the back of the houses and toward Buckman's so he could check on his brother. He found John sitting on the ground near the tavern's stables, with his head bowed in his hands. John was trembling.

"Are you all right?" Nathaniel asked his brother.

"I'm fine, Nathaniel, but angry and sad. Did you see what they did to our friends and neighbors?"

Nathaniel took several deep breaths, trying to calm himself, and gathered his thoughts about their next moves. He sat next to his brother and reassured him, "Today is not over. They have to come back by here at some point. We all need to find some revenge for what just happened. But we need to get the rest of the family to safety."

John jumped up. "If we get approval from Captain Parker, I'll let them know what has happened and have them leave as soon as they can."

They went inside to speak to Captain Parker, who was meeting with many of the surviving militiamen, getting their opinions on what to do next. "Men, we need to decide our next moves," Nathaniel heard him saying.

Nathaniel asked him, "Can we check on our families while the Regulars march on to Concord?"

"Yes, men. Any of you who live nearby can make a brief visit to let your family members know that you're safe. Come back here quickly, as we'll be heading to the Lincoln line to meet the Regulars on their return trip. I'll have some of you stay here to protect the town."

Nathaniel stayed with the men who did not need to leave or had multiple family members on site. He sent John back again to let the family know what had happened and to remind their brother, Sam, get the family out of town to the safe site they had previously arranged.

Chapter 10

April 19, 1775
Morning

The deadly events on the Green had not gone unnoticed by Lydia. She and Mary had sat motionless and silent in the darkness as rows and rows of shadowy figures passed by just outside their windows. As dawn approached, Lydia followed at a safe distance behind the last lines of Regulars as they marched into the center of town. She stayed back on the slope going toward the Green long enough to hear the frightening volleys as shots were fired. The sound of gunfire made her tremble, knowing her brothers were possible targets. She could not see the green from her vantage point, but the sounds were enough to frighten her. Immediately she turned and headed home, realizing that the family had to get out of there and to someplace safer. She lifted her skirt and ran as fast as she could away from the skirmish, hoping Nathaniel and John were not harmed.

At the house, her mother was waiting at the door. "What did you see?" she asked, her voice full of concern and fear.

"Shots were fired, Mother. I don't know what happened, but as John had said, we can't stay here, at least for the day. The Regulars are shooting at townspeople and may come back this way. We are not safe here until we know the fighting is over."

"But what about your brothers? I'm afraid they may have been hit with the shots that were fired."

Lydia hadn't seen her mother this upset for some time. As she was trying to think of what they should do next, Sam pulled the wagon around to the front of the house, which was what John had instructed him to do before returning to the Green.

"We have to get the family to the Latham's house in Woburn as planned," Sam said. "Mary, help me get Rebeckah and Joseph ready. Lydia, finish putting the supplies into the back of the wagon. I'm going to smother the fire in the fireplace and get everything closed up."

He had just finished speaking when his mother let out a scream. "John! Thank the Lord you are all right! Where is Nathaniel?"

John had come up the road, running, to let the family know what had happened. "Nathaniel is fine. The Regulars shot at us, Mother! Several men are dead, including Caleb, and many are wounded, but Nathaniel and I were not harmed. It was terrible, and I'm afraid for you if you stay here. You must all leave, NOW!"

The family climbed into the wagon after supplies were loaded; they took whatever they could and what they needed, not knowing how long they would be gone. John hugged his mother and brother, put his hand on Lydia's shoulder, and headed back into town. Sam sat on the bench in front with Rebeckah, who was clutching her doll and some crewel work she treasured. Lydia and Mary sat with their mother in back with Joseph who was playing with a fife. The two youngest were oblivious to what had happened in town and thought they were going on a grand adventure.

Lydia thought to herself, *What is happening to our simple life? Will we all be all right after this terrible day? Those poor people in town with family members dead or dying.* She thought back to the hardships the family had dealt with when her father had died eight years before; it had made them all more dependent on each other and stronger individually, but she knew it had been easier having the many townspeople willing to help them. Now many of those same townspeople were dealing with tragedy and fear. With the concerns of war and the struggles all the colonies might endure, the hardships this time would be different.

The old, creaky wagon began the ride north to Woburn, being passed by many armed militiamen from other towns heading toward the Green. Mrs. Mulliken looked at Lydia with deep concern on her

CHAPTER 10

face. She was worried sick about her two sons and hoped the rest of them would be safe for the rest of this troubling day and through the night, until they could once again be home together. They could not imagine what was ahead as they slowly made their way out of Lexington, watching their house fade into the distance.

Meanwhile, the Regulars finished their march to Concord. As they reached Concord center, Major Pitcairn and Colonel Smith climbed one of the highest spots in town, located in the burying ground across from Wright's Tavern, to survey what lay ahead of them. After reviewing a map drafted by a Loyalist for General Gage, the major used his spyglass and looked down on the center of Concord, then toward the two bridges that provided access into town.

"Lieutenant," Pitcairn yelled to one of the officers down on the road. "Send one of your men up here and to cut down this blasted liberty pole."

"Yes, sir." The officer pointed to one of the grenadiers, who took his hatchet from his belt and climbed the hill. In a few minutes, the liberty pole was down.

The two commanding officers went back down to the main road. After discussing strategy with Colonel Smith, Pitcairn called for two of the officers. "Captain Pole and Lieutenant Parsons, come here." When the officers rode up on their horses, he gave them their orders. "Captain Pole, take your men to the South Bridge. Parsons, take your men to the North Bridge." He pointed out both locations on his map. "Defend the bridges. Parsons, send part of your group to the Barrett Farm. Find and destroy any weapons. We have reports from spies that there should be many at that location."

"Yes, sir," both officers replied.

"Do not destroy or damage any personal property," Pitcairn told the men assigned for those missions before they marched out of town.

Pitcairn and Colonel Smith stayed in town, overseeing the search-and-destroy mission of military goods that might be found there based upon intelligence gathered previously from Loyalists in town. They found nothing worthwhile at Reuben Brown's harness shop or Samuel Barrett's gun shop. At Ebenezer Hubbard's malthouse, they pulled out a few barrels of flour and dumped the small barrels into the street. Larger ones were rolled into the millpond.

Major Pitcairn accompanied a group of grenadiers as they went into an inn/town jail to search for hidden supplies. Ephraim Jones, the owner, confronted them, stating it was private property and refused to open the door. Pitcairn ordered one of the grenadiers to break it down, and the force of the large man easily opened the door. Upon entering and being blocked by the innkeeper, the major knocked him down, put one of his pistols to the man's head, and demanded they be shown what was hidden there.

Ephraim had no choice; he showed the grenadiers a couple of cannons hidden in the backyard, as well as a few barrels of musket balls in another part of the property. The cannons were spiked and the trunnions that were used to move them broken off, making them useless. The barrels of musket balls were dumped into the millpond out back. The wheels of the cannon carriages were piled on the ground in front of the meetinghouse, together with other supplies they had found. Once the rest of the building was searched, Major Pitcairn told Ephraim he would order breakfast for the men and offered to pay full price. They stopped their search work temporarily to enjoy a quick meal.

When the searches were completed, Pitcairn and Smith had all the goods they had seized added to the pile outside the meetinghouse and had them set afire. As the flames grew, some of the embers landed on the roof of the meetinghouse, and it started to smoke.

"Stop!" yelled Martha Moulton as she ran over to the soldiers, struggling to carry a wooden bucket of water. "Are you going to burn down the town?"

"No, just these illegal items," said Pitcairn.

"The meetinghouse will burn unless you stop it now," the widow insisted.

"Calm down, madam," Pitcairn told her. He ordered some of the men to gather some buckets and take some water from the mill pond and extinguish the smoldering roof of the meetinghouse.

CHAPTER 10

Satisfied with their efforts, Martha waved her hands at them in disgust and returned to her home.

At the North Bridge, the royal troops that had been sent there had a skirmish with colonists; the first casualties of the war were inflicted on the Regulars by a large force of minutemen protecting the bridge. The light infantry was outnumbered, pushed back, and retreated into town. As they came into the center of town, they spoke of the withering attack they had faced. Some of the wounded men were treated quickly at Wright's Tavern or Dr. Minot's in the center of town. A couple of wagons and small carriages were seized from local homes and used to transport those who could not walk. Colonel Smith ordered the forces to assemble so they could start the march back toward Boston, but they had difficulty getting everyone into formation and waited for the forces returning from Colonel Barrett's or those who had protected the South Bridge.

To the dismay and horror of the soldiers and officers, some of the men returning had frightening stories that spread throughout the forces of wounded soldiers being mangled or harmed by colonists. They had seen what they thought were acts of cruelty upon many of the wounded, even though many were being helped by colonists and local doctors. In reality, one of the soldiers wounded at the bridge had tried to get up as the militia passed, chasing the Regulars back into town. A young boy in the group thought the wounded man was threatening to him, so he struck him with a hatchet, putting the soldier out of his misery. But the stories made the remaining troops very nervous and also anxious as they prepared to march. The sight of a growing number of the militia starting to cross fields and come over nearby hills made that concern grow even deeper.

Colonel Smith waited to make sure all his men were in formation, were sufficiently prepared for the march back to Boston, and the wounded were able to travel. He had the officers pass among the men with words of encouragement. Then, after much delay, they began the long march back to Boston after noon.

As soon as the redcoats were out of sight along Lexington Road, the townspeople went about repairing any damage done by the Regulars during their searches. The next day, Amos Melvin, Reuben

Brown, and David Suttle joined other men who dredged the millpond, where the soldiers had thrown any musket balls that had been found. Most of those musket balls were recovered, along with several barrels of flour that had sealed up from the water, and were still useful.

Chapter 11

April 19, 1775
Morning

As the spring sun rose on the horizon, Samuel reached the town of Stow, starting to feel tired from a long night. He was seeing more and more militiamen, some individually, many in groups, passing by him going in the opposite direction as he rode through town. Word seemed to be preceding him and his message as he heard the continual sound of muskets firing and church bells ringing in surrounding villages, sounding the alarm. Satisfied that the news was being heard, he stopped at a small farm pond along the road, dismounted to rest for just a moment, and let Rascal drink from the pond. It had been a long but rewarding night as he felt he had helped get the message out early to many of the surrounding militia groups. One group of men from Lancaster stopped to ask Samuel what he knew.

"I left Lexington about midnight, and the men there were preparing to meet the Regulars as they marched on their way to Concord. I believe the target is Concord's supply of weapons."

The men tipped their hats at Samuel and continued toward Concord.

After they passed, Samuel climbed back onto the horse, turned back toward Concord, and headed home. When he crossed the Concord town line, back into an area he knew well, Samuel decided it might be wise to avoid the center of town in the event the Regulars were already there searching homes and buildings. He took a left turn onto Barrett's Mill Road, just west of the center, so he could bypass town by going over the North Bridge.

As Samuel approached Colonel Barrett's farm, he noticed far ahead of him a group of about a hundred soldiers marching up the road. He quickly veered into a large group of pine trees just after Colonel Barrett's fields so they could pass without seeing him. He waited and peered through the thick pine branches, stroking Rascal's neck to keep him quiet. The soldiers hurried by, in full uniform, muskets on their shoulders. Samuel thought to himself, *It was a good thing Amos and the other men moved those supplies out of town.*

Once the procession had passed and were far enough away not to notice him, Samuel guided Rascal quietly back onto the path. Crossing Lowell Road, he heard sporadic musket firing from the area near the bridge up ahead and then several loud volleys which startled Rascal. Samuel paused, trying to decide if he should continue forward or cut back toward town. His mind was not as sharp as usual from being up all night, but he decided if there was firing up ahead, his medical skills might be needed. He spurred Rascal into a gallop and headed toward the bridge and Major Buttrick's house.

Once he was closer to Major Buttrick's, Samuel saw the masses of men and a lot of activity, with many different groups moving in several directions. Looking across the bridge, he saw the rear lines of the Regular troops running back up from the bridge and turning toward town. A group of colonists were on the bridge itself, and there were several groups of militiamen in the field on the left; several other groups were in Reverend Emerson's field on the right, firing as the redcoats marched past. Reverend Emerson himself was walking among the men on Samuel's side of the bridge, shouting encouragement and support.

A group of men were carrying two of the militiamen away from the bridge, toward Samuel. He saw Captain Robbins with them and asked him what had happened.

"Tragic day, Dr. Prescott. One of our captains, Isaac Davis, and one of our men, Abner Hosmer, were killed on the bridge as we moved forward. We're taking them to the Buttrick house. I just sent

CHAPTER 11

two of my men to let Hannah and their four children know." The group passed with the two dead men.

Samuel also saw several men on his side of the bridge lying on the ground, being tended to, and he recognized Doctor Minot as one of the people helping the wounded men. He rode up and asked how he could help.

"Samuel, we've taken care of those who were most seriously hurt, and two of the Acton men were killed instantly. It's too dangerous to go into town, but can you offer the wounded here some assistance?" asked Dr. Minot.

"Yes, sir, of course." Samuel tied Rascal to a tree and went to one of the wounded men lying in the field. He was approached by Reverend Emerson.

"How can I help?" Samuel was asked by the reverend.

"Just help me clean his wound. I will need some water and some cloth to wrap it afterwards." Samuel was pleased to have the reverend by his side and asked him, "What happened here?"

"I was standing in my field watching it unfold," Reverend Emerson recalled. "The Regulars had split up with a group of them continuing toward Colonel Barrett's farm while the rest stayed on the other side of the bridge to stop anyone from crossing."

"Yes, I passed the group going to Barrett's. Go on," Samuel said.

"The hill above the bridge continued to fill with militia coming in from some neighboring towns, the numbers growing substantially. The Regulars retreated over the bridge, but some stopped and tried to remove a few of the planks. After being warned by the militia, the soldiers stopped and formed ranks on my side of the bridge. The militia troops started to march down the hill, and the Regulars grouped in firing position, with some kneeling and others positioned standing behind them. When the militia reached the bridge, the redcoats fired. I saw two of the men in front go down, then the militia returned a heavy fire. Several of the redcoats fell. Both sides continued firing until the Regulars realized they were outnumbered and began retreating toward town."

Samuel shook his head. "This is terrible, but not unexpected. The other group will be coming back this way shortly. Help me care for this man."

The young minuteman groaned and was trembling, saying he was frightened. "Am I going to die, sir? I am so afraid. I don't want to leave my young wife and children alone."

"Nonsense, young man," Samuel said. "We will take care of this for you. You have many more healthy days ahead of you." He was trying to reassure the young man.

"But those two Acton men are gone. They left their homes and families this morning and now will never return. It all happened so quickly. We saw smoke rising from the center of town and thought the Regulars might be burning it down, so we were ordered to move forward."

"Shh—just stay calm. Life is very precious, and you must keep still. When you get home to your family, treasure every moment with them. How many children do you have?" Samuel used a small set of forceps from his bag to find and remove the musket ball in the man's shoulder, cleaned the wound with fresh water brought to him by Reverend Emerson, pressed firmly on it until the bleeding stopped, then wrapped it carefully to keep it dry. He used extra cloth to form a sling to immobilize the arm.

"I have a son and a daughter, sir. They are very young." The man started to sob.

"You will have stories to tell them when they are older. They will be proud that their father was here today and fought for their safety and protection. There, you are all set. Get rest until this heals, and then you will be ready to fight another day. I'm afraid, after today, there will be many days ahead for more fighting."

He asked some of the militiamen and women nearby to gently help the young man to Major Buttrick's house so he could rest.

"What is your name, young man?" Samuel asked as the man stood and was helped by several bystanders.

"David, David Quimby. Thank you, Doctor."

As David was led away, Reverend Emerson stood next to Samuel. "Well done, Dr. Prescott, well done," said Reverend Emerson. "You

CHAPTER 11

helped him physically, but even more so spiritually. Saving lives is your calling."

"We help people in similar ways, Reverend. Your words can also save lives. I've seen how you have inspired people to make the most out of their daily lives. I may fix broken bones, but your words can mend broken souls. I can fix wounds with stitches and bandages, but you can put together the spirit and faith in people with just the right inspirational phrase. And by the way, thank you for your help."

The two shook hands and then went to see if there was anything else that they could do to help any injured men. Dr. Minot and the few doctors who had been part of the militia groups from several of the towns finally had things under control and thanked Samuel.

The militia groups were organizing as they were aware the Barrett farm search company would be returning to cross back over the bridge. Samuel stopped one of the officers from the Groton forces.

"Excuse me, sir. Have you heard any news from Lexington regarding the Regulars marching through there this morning?"

"I'm afraid there was an encounter with men from that town, and there are reports of many dead and wounded among the townspeople," the officer replied, shaking his head in sorrow.

This news terrified Samuel, thinking of the Mulliken brothers who were there. He ran to Rascal and mounted him.

"Samuel, be careful. The Regulars are still in town," warned Reverend Emerson.

"Thank you. I'll go over Ripley Hill to my house to avoid town. I need to check on my family and then get to Lexington." He turned Rascal's head toward the bridge, and as he approached it, he glanced to his left, where several of the militia were cleaning their muskets and changing flints in preparation for a potential battle ahead. They were on the very spot where he had set the quilt on that June day the year before, to sit there with Lydia. It caught him off guard for a moment, but he refocused, spurred the horse over the bridge and up the hill, taking a route that would keep him parallel to Lexington Road until he could come down the ridge behind his house.

Chapter 12

April 19, 1775
Late morning through afternoon

Samuel descended the other side of Ripley Hill behind their house, surprised by the scores of men from nearby towns that he saw following along the ridge behind him. It was almost noon, and the column of Regulars had not yet started down his street, but it looked like they were going to face some resistance as more and more militiamen were arriving each minute.

Samuel set Rascal into his stall and ran into the house. His father and Benjamin were packing some supplies while his mother, Abigail, and sister, Lucy, wrapped china in cloth before boxing it.

"Samuel!" his mother shouted. "Thank the Lord you're safe."

"Has Abel returned yet?" Samuel asked his father.

"Not yet. He was more rested than you and may have decided to go further with the alarm."

All of them gathered around him and asked what he had seen.

"I avoided a company of Regulars searching Colonel Barrett's, then arrived at the North Bridge soon after a battle there had ended. At least two local men had been killed by the troops, who were fired upon and retreated into town after suffering casualties themselves."

Samuel helped his father and Benjamin move some goods into the barn.

Not far from the Prescott house, the Royal Army officers continued preparing their men for the march back to Boston, making sure they had gathered some water and food to help them on their

CHAPTER 12

return trip, as well as ensuring the wounded men had safe transportation on carriages they had seized. Finally, about noon, the order was given to march. Major Pitcairn and some of the junior officers led the assembled group as they left the center of town. Pitcairn ordered many of the light infantry to send out some flankers to protect the sides of the column, as well as to protect the rear of the march. Slowly they made their way back toward Boston, not realizing what they were about to encounter.

The Prescott family knew the troops were going to pass their house as they left town. Samuel asked his father what they should do.

The older Prescott looked concerned. "The redcoats will be marching out of town any minute now since they've finished searching here and have seen the resistance. They'll be coming right by here shortly."

As Samuel helped Lucy secure some of the plates, he heard activity outside. He went to the window facing the center of town and saw the first lines of soldiers headed toward his house.

"Here they come!" Samuel ran to the front door and locked it while Benjamin pushed a chest in front of it.

They stood to the sides of the front windows and watched as officers on horses, a wagon with injured troops, and the front line of larger grenadiers starting to pass. They saw flankers occasionally run into yards or within fences or walls of neighboring homes. The long line of the column slowly and steadily passed, never stopping at the Prescott house, more intent on getting back to Boston.

"I think we're all right," his father said after they passed. "Let's try to get everything back in order."

They were almost done putting things away when they heard rapid hoofbeats outside and someone yelling.

"Dr. Prescott! Dr. Prescott!" the young man shouted. "Your brother has been shot!"

Samuel unbolted the door and swung it open. Outside, looking stunned and desperate, was Jacob Walker.

"What? Jacob, what happened?" Samuel asked.

"He was returning over the South Bridge this morning, and one of the Regulars who was guarding the bridge shot him. We carried your brother into Mrs. Heyward's house."

"Benjamin and Samuel, grab your bags and supplies," their father ordered. "All of us have to help Abel."

All three doctors—Abel Sr., Benjamin, and Samuel—went outside to get their horses. Mrs. Prescott had her hand over her mouth while Lucy sat in a chair, crying.

"Mother, we'll take care of him. We'll send Samuel back once we know the extent of Abel's injuries," Benjamin yelled as they mounted and headed out.

The three men galloped back through town and to Mrs. Heyward's house, a spot all three had been to before to help her with several illnesses. The house was on a small hill a short distance from the South Bridge, overlooking the Concord River below.

They rushed inside and found Abel Jr. lying on a bed in a back room. He was fortunately awake, responsive, and very pleased to see them, smiling with a slight grimace as they entered the room.

"Praise the Lord. I get three doctors at one time," he said.

"Are you all right, Abel?" Samuel asked.

"Just shot in the side, Samuel, but I don't think it is that serious. It knocked me off my horse, but I believe we've stopped the bleeding."

Samuel watched as his father checked the wound, which had been cleaned by Mrs. Heyward after instructions from Abel Jr.

"It looks better than we thought," his father said, relieved. "Benjamin and I will take care of Abel, Samuel. Get back and reassure your mother and sister that he'll be okay. We'll stay with him for the night, if Mrs. Heyward doesn't mind."

"Of course, Dr. Prescott. Do whatever you need to take care of your son," she said.

Samuel touched his brother on his shoulder, nodded to his father and Benjamin, and went home to soothe his mother and Lucy. They were waiting for him as he rode up to the house.

"Please tell me he's okay, Samuel," his mother said.

CHAPTER 12

"He has a wound on his left side, but Father and Benjamin are treating it. They'll spend the night to keep an eye on him. He should be okay if it heals properly."

Mrs. Prescott and Lucy were so relieved to hear that Abel Jr. was not seriously injured.

Knowing everyone in the Prescott house was now content and satisfied that the danger of the Regulars had passed, Samuel went back to worrying about the events in Lexington and the effects on the Mullikens, knowing Nathaniel and John were involved. A deeper concern was Lydia's well-being, as Samuel did not know how the assault by the Regulars might have affected the family.

Since the retreating soldiers had had enough time to march several miles ahead of him, he felt comfortable to be on the same road, a distance behind them. He guided Duchess across the small Mill Brook Bridge in front of Nathan Meriam's house and began to see what an ongoing battle it had been for the Regulars leaving Concord. He saw several wounded or dead redcoat soldiers, many being helped by townspeople. He stopped to offer help but was told they had everything under control. It was even more alarming as he approached the same Hartwell Tavern, where he had stopped earlier that morning, as the crooked nature of the road slowed down the retreat, allowing a more-deadly attack by the militia as the redcoats tried to pass. There were many more dead and wounded soldiers in that section of the road. He saw Mary Hartwell on the side of the road bent over a wounded man and stopped to talk to her.

"Mrs. Hartwell, how can I help?"

"Well, young man, I see your warnings were right. Thank you for asking, but it is too late for this man," she replied, pulling a blanket over the man's face. "Keep going. There will be many more opportunities to help along this road."

Samuel nodded and spurred Duchess on to Lexington.

CHAPTER 13

April 19, 1775
Midmorning

The ride over the dirt road was bumpy, knocking the passengers around, and it seemed to last forever even though it was just slightly over an hour. Sam guided the horses around a few holes and dips in the road while Mary noted how more and more militiamen seemed to be passing them.

"Where are they all going?" she asked to no one in particular.

"Probably heading to Lexington or Concord," said Sam. "Responding to alarms from during the night."

As the trip proceeded, Lydia looked up and saw ahead of them a large white farmhouse with a good-sized grey barn on the right side.

"This is the place that Elijah had planned for us in case we needed to get out of town for the day," Sam told his family. "Guess it's a distant cousin of his, who Nathaniel has used for some clock hardware in the past."

As the wagon bounced up to the front of the farmhouse, a mountain of a man with grey hair and a well-trimmed grey beard came rushing out of the door to meet them.

"Hello, Mullikens!" he bellowed. "Myles Latham. It's a pleasure to meet you all."

They climbed off the wagon, and Mrs. Mulliken introduced her children. "Mr. Latham, this is my son, Sam, daughters, Lydia and Mary, and the youngsters are Rebeckah and Joseph."

CHAPTER 13

"What a great family! Nathaniel told me he had brothers and sisters but never said they were such a handsome group. Hah!" he shouted.

He was one of the largest men Lydia had ever seen, close to seven feet tall with broad shoulders and large arms.

"Please come inside to meet my wife, Prudence," Latham said.

They entered the house and were met with the smells of cinnamon and roasting meat. A petite woman with grey hair tied up in a very neat bun smiled widely as they walked into the room. She walked over to meet them, leaning to her left and walking with a cane.

"We're so happy we can help, especially under these circumstances. We heard what happened in the village from some of the men as they passed," she said.

"Your brothers were wise to have a good plan in place in case of a situation like this," Myles told Lydia. "Please, sit and relax for a while."

Myles looked at Joseph, who was hiding a wooden fife in his right hand, behind his back. "Young Mr. Mulliken, is that a fife?"

"Yes, sir," Joseph mumbled.

"Hah! Let me see. I can play for you."

Joseph looked at his mother for approval, and when she nodded, he slowly handed the fife to Mr. Latham. To everyone's surprise, Latham played a beautiful short melody, something they didn't expect with such soft music coming from this large man. When finished, Myles gave the fife back to Joseph.

"Haven't done that for a while." He laughed loudly. "And, Miss Rebeckah, is that an instrument you are holding as well?"

"No, sir, just some crewel I'm working on." She held out a piece of white material; the letters R and M were stitched in black.

"RM? Hmm. What could those stand for?" mused Myles. "Let me guess. Remington Morningside?" He had a mischievous twinkle in his eyes.

"No." Rebeckah giggled.

"I thought that was it for sure. Maybe Regina Mecklenberger?"

"No, it's Rebeckah Mulliken."

"Hah! I should have known." Myles laughed so hard they thought the walls shook.

Prudence put some cider and cinnamon bread on the table. As Mrs. Mulliken, Lydia, and Mary sat with her, Sam went out to secure the horses. Myles stood beside and slightly behind his wife, placing his right hand on her left shoulder.

Looking at Lydia, he spoke with a very soft tone in his voice for such a big man. "I truly admire what your brothers are doing. Would be in front of the line with them if I could. But we have no family, no one nearby to help Prudence. Since her illness several years ago, she needs me around the house more than the cause of liberty does." He gently caressed her shoulder, and she looked up at him, smiling, as she put her hand on his.

Then he laughed and said to Rebeckah and Joseph, "I want to introduce you to some of my friends." He winked at the women as he passed, whispering, "I'll keep the little ones entertained so not to worry them through all of this."

His wife touched his arm as he passed before turning to Lydia, Mary, and their mother. "We've never been able to have children, but he loves making them smile."

Myles brought the two children outside to a fenced area behind the house.

"Meet my friends, Rufus and Erasmus," he said proudly, pointing inside the fence.

"Those are goats!" said Joseph.

"Really? Can't they still be my friends? Hah!"

They all laughed. Myles gave them some carrots to feed the goats

Inside, Prudence tried to reassure Mrs. Mulliken and her daughters.

"Hopefully, the worst is over. Your sons are safe, and you're welcome to spend the night here comfortably until your town is cleared. We have plenty of food and enough room."

"Thank you, Prudence," said Mrs. Mulliken. "You and Myles are so kind to shelter us until we can return home tomorrow."

CHAPTER 13

"He's such a good man—loud sometimes, but a good, generous man. He knew your husband well, apprenticed with him as a blacksmith before Nathaniel went to study under Benjamin Willard as a clockmaker. Myles's large hands and boundless energy weren't designed for the delicate task of building clocks. I believe your husband and, eventually, your son, Nathaniel, used some of the metal hardware he has created. Elijah has also been having him make pieces for his cabinets."

"I remember my husband speaking of a very skilled blacksmith who was a remarkable man—loud and boisterous, but gentle and compassionate."

For the remainder of the day, the women made the house ready and comfortable for everyone to share the space. Prudence would sleep on a day bed in the main room while Myles and Sam slept on the floor in front of the fireplace. Mrs. Mulliken was graciously given the Latham's room, and Rebeckah and Joseph would join her, sleeping on blankets on the floor. Lydia and Mary were given the small room in the back used for guests.

As Lydia and Mary prepared for bed, they spoke about the events of the day, their concern for their brothers, and the kindness of the Lathams.

"I'll be so glad to get home, and see Nathaniel and John. I just want know we're all safe," Mary said as she climbed into bed.

Lydia nodded. "Yes, and I hope my Samuel will send word of what happened in Concord."

"Mr. Latham is such a nice man, but if I hear another '*hah*,' I think I'll scream!" said Mary.

Lydia chuckled.

Myles was heard in the other room, laughing with Sam, near the fireplace. "Hah!" he bellowed.

Mary looked at Lydia, rolled her eyes, and they both laughed. Lydia reached over and blew out the candle in their room. It had been a very troubling, stressful day, but the welcome shown by the Lathams and the lighter mood provided by the humor from Myles gave them some peace. Soon they were asleep.

Chapter 14

April 19, 1775
Late morning

Back in Lexington, Captain Parker had gathered his men. They had come to grips with what had happened to them that dawn. Many of them were stunned and shocked after seeing friends and relatives killed or wounded. They asked Captain Parker how they should respond to the terrible events that had unfolded. Some wanted to just go home, but many wanted to pursue the Regulars as they marched on to Concord.

Captain Parker stayed calm, telling them, "We cannot do that. It would be foolish, as we are so outnumbered. We need time to allow men from other towns to answer the alarm and decide how to proceed." After discussions with the oldest men in the group, Parker let them all know his plans.

"Men, we know the Regulars have to come back through town. We don't want them having it as easy as they did this morning, and we cannot let them use the town Green to attack us again. We will have the advantage if we march out to a position of advantage on Fiske Hill, where we can ambush them before they know we are there. Many of you are grieving or angry. We have all felt a growing resentment of our treatment from the king. Will we let this be a simple victory for the Regulars? Or will we make a stand for our loved ones and this town we all represent? Who is with me?"

Unanimously, the men shouted their approval. While everyone wanted to be part of this revenge on the Regulars, it was decided that

CHAPTER 14

some of them should remain in town. They could protect against any possible reinforcements that General Gage might send out from Boston; and they could be there to instruct militia groups from other towns on what positions along the way would be most advantageous for attack. Already, a large group from Woburn had arrived, eager to assist where needed. Captain Parker chose the men he wanted to take with him. Nathaniel would go with the forward group while John would stay in town.

"Be safe, brother," John said as Nathaniel joined the group about to march.

As the Lexington men started out, the bodies of the men killed that morning were put in wooden coffins inside the meetinghouse. A short while later, they were taken to the Old Burying Ground and put in a common grave. Worried that the Regulars might pass by on the way back to Boston and discover and disturb the grave, Reverend Clarke had some men cover it with brush.

The Lexington militia followed Captain Parker out of town, heading west; William Diamond accompanied them with his drum while fifer Jonathan Harrington, younger cousin of the other Jonathan who had died, played a fife. As the group approached the Lincoln line, they climbed the bluff overlooking the main road and took their position. While they hid behind trees, brush, and large stones, Nathaniel thought back to earlier that morning. His fear and uncertainty at that time had been replaced with an intense hatred and a fierce determination for revenge.

Lifelong friends and neighbors had been shot at his side, and the cheering of the Regulars still echoed in his mind. He could still hear Jonathan Harrington's groans and see a distraught Ruth Harrington rushing to her husband's side as he crawled to the foot of their front steps. Waiting next to Nathaniel, old Jebediah Munroe, who was wounded on the Green earlier, was ready for battle. There was a rag wrapped around Jebediah's arm, dried blood visible; the right side of his face still had black ash on it from firing his musket twice that morning. Several other men had black powder stains on their shirts. Nathaniel realized he would never, ever hesitate to shoot a soldier of the king's army now. He saw them as a true enemy, and he longed for the opportunity to fight back.

He wouldn't have to wait long. The sound of musketry growing closer in front of them brought his mind back into focus. The columns of troops were closing in on their position, running as they approached. Many of the redcoat officers were on horseback, shouting orders. The midday sun shining through leafless branches was shaded by smoke from the muskets drifting up into the trees. Nathaniel could see other militia running into pine groves on opposite sides of the road, loading their weapons as they reached a firing spot. His own musket was already loaded, with the lock pulled back. Nathaniel raised the musket to his eye as the soldiers came into view, and he pushed back his hat for a clearer view. This time, as the enemy drew near, his heart beat with anticipation. His finger on his right hand stroked the trigger up and down several times as he anticipated the order to fire. Then he waited, as Captain Parker had ordered them, and waited. And waited. It seemed like hours as the column passed right before them.

"Fire!" Captain Parker shouted, and the entire Lexington company let loose a barrage of musket balls. Nathaniel picked out the nearest red uniform and carefully squeezed the trigger. The gun fired, and through the smoke, he saw the soldier fall. Quickly he pulled another cartridge out, primed and loaded his musket, and fired again. This time he missed.

The smell of powder filled the air. Men on both sides were yelling instructions and encouragement. The crying and moaning of the injured was drowned out by the firing of muskets.

From Nathaniel's right, a group of Regulars was trying to dislodge the minutemen from the hill by attacking from the side. Jebediah Munroe, fighting until the end, was struck by a musket ball and fell. Nathaniel saw several other Lexington men fall. Other militiamen would move away, then stop, fire, and move again. The flankers were coming his way from both sides now.

His cartridge box was almost empty. Nathaniel jumped up just as a musket ball struck the rock in front of him, throwing shattered pieces of granite into the air. Time to move! He ran back from the

CHAPTER 14

roadway and over the ridge, taking a path he knew from hunting trips with his father, and he made his way back toward Lexington. He was certain John had stored some extra ammunition for him in the back of the clock shop. He knew this day was far from over, and he needed more cartridges.

In the meantime, Major Pitcairn was dealing with problems with his own forces as they retreated. They had been followed relentlessly from Concord, under continuous fire, with members of the militia from many towns arriving and lining their route to Boston. Along with fellow officers, he had ordered flankers to spread out to dislodge the enemy where possible, but the task grew more difficult as the number of militiamen swelled. Casualties continued to increase, and the morale and usual discipline of the infantry faltered. The major became more alarmed as some of the men were actually running in fear and breaking from their orderly formation.

Trying to gain some control of his forces, Pitcairn trotted his horse to the front of the masses of men, turned to face them, and raised one of his treasured pistols over his head. "Come to order! Remain in formation!" he shouted, trying desperately to be heard above the sound of musket fire and the yelling of other officers. "Any man who breaks rank and separates will be shot on the spot!" Then he fired the pistol into the air to make his point. It caught their attention and at least temporarily brought back the order and discipline he expected from the Regulars. He returned his pistol to his saddlebag, withdrawing his sword instead.

As they climbed Fiske's Bluff, Pitcairn rode back and forth in front of his men, shouting encouragement and urging them on. Suddenly a shot from behind one of the stone walls grazed the back of his horse. Having received a minor wound on Lexington Green, the horse was spooked this time, causing it to throw Pitcairn. He hit the ground hard but quickly got up and, now horseless, joined the lines of infantrymen passing by. As the horse galloped away, it jumped a stone wall and was stopped by several militiamen, one of them grabbing its reins and calming it down. The man removed the saddlebag and was surprised to find the two elegant silver pistols that meant so much to the major.

He yelled out to one of his officers, "Sir, look what I just found." He handed the pistols to the officer.

"Well done, soldier. Get that horse out of here. I'll put these away until our fight is over."

Meanwhile, back in Lexington, Nathaniel was breathless as he came within sight of the Green. So much had happened since he stood there that morning. Those killed and wounded had been removed, and it looked peaceful despite what was happening around him. Nathaniel thought back to how he had waited that morning for the same troops he was now fighting. His path home ran parallel to the running Regulars, so he kept his distance. Everywhere he looked, he saw militia companies joining those already in pursuit. Nathaniel was pleased so many other towns had joined forces with those in his town. He knew John would be among them.

On both sides of the road, muskets were still firing at the column of soldiers, who appeared exhausted. Many of them were collapsing from fatigue; others were hanging on the edge of the wagons carrying the wounded. Some were seen clinging to the sides of officers' horses. Their pace had slowed from when he had seen them earlier. *They will never make it back to Boston!* Nathaniel thought.

Suddenly an enormous blast in front of him stopped him. He looked up to see a cannonball crash through both the front and rear walls of the meetinghouse on the Green. Splinters of wood came flying into the air, scattering on the ground around the rear of the meetinghouse. Everyone stopped momentarily to see what had happened before the Regulars let out a loud cheer, realizing they had been rescued by reinforcements. Another loud blast from the cannon followed.

Gathering his senses, Nathaniel decided to circle around the village to his house. He was concerned now about his mother, sisters, and younger brothers and hoped they had left as planned. He wanted to get a better view of what was happening near the house.

As Nathaniel approached their house, he saw that the reinforcements were stationed almost directly in front of his property. The Regulars had set up a picket line to the left of his land, facing the center of town, another line was in front of him, and a third parallel

CHAPTER 14

to this one. They basically surrounded the road on three sides. Fresh soldiers were mingling with the exhausted group they had just rescued. The wounded were being carried or moved down the road to the Munroe Tavern, not far from his house.

Taking a route that he had traveled many times through the fields and around the hill behind the house, he made his way to their rear pastures.

Nathaniel sat on the cold ground, trying to figure out how he could get through the lines to the clock shop, visible from that distance. He needed more ammunition. To his relief, there was no activity close to the house, so it appeared the family must have left before the reinforcements had arrived. Meanwhile, an occasional musket fired at the Regulars from the many militiamen facing the lines. He waited there for some time, catching his breath and contemplating his next move.

During this time, the battered and exhausted Regulars collapsed within the protection set up by their reinforcements. It had been almost fourteen hours of marching, intense fighting, and little rest. They laid on the roadside or on lawns in front of houses along the roadway. General Hugh Percy, who had led the reinforcements, and his officers had taken over Munroe Tavern and set it up as a field hospital. Many of the troops were sprawled out on the grass outside, exhausted. After checking on the condition of their men, Major Pitcairn and Colonel Smith went to report to Percy on what they had been dealing with since leaving Concord.

"Looks like you encountered some difficulties along the way," stated Percy. "Good thing you had requested reinforcements. Are there many provincials out there?"

"There are more and more men streaming in from other towns," Colonel Smith said. "You saved us from being completely overwhelmed by the rebels."

"And they all have a way of finding fences, walls, or trees to hide behind, too cowardly to come out and fight," said Pitcairn. "They are even shooting at us from inside or behind houses. We're in an unsafe position with those three houses nearby."

General Percy looked at the area around them, grasped the situation, and called out to one of his junior officers. "Lieutenant! Gather some of your men and check the three houses on each side of us. Make sure no one is in them, then burn them down."

"Yes, sir!" The young man saluted and started giving orders to several of his men.

From the rear pastures of his property, Nathaniel decided it might be best to circle back to town and find his brother, John. And then he saw it—smoke! He stood up, peering more closely at the house. He saw a sight that made him sick inside—*their house was on fire*. Soon the dark smoke turned to flames. It poured out the windows on the first floor and licked the outside walls. The black smoke kept getting thicker, and the flames grew larger. He could see the small clock shop also burning next to the house. The hurt and anger grew inside him. All his father's hard work and the many hours Nathaniel himself had spent keeping the shop going were being burned away before his eyes.

For a moment, driven by emotion, Nathaniel wanted to drop his musket and run right through the line of soldiers, but common sense overruled his anger and despair. The family home started to crumble and fall from the fire, and Nathaniel had to turn and look away. For the first time, he realized he was crying, harder than he had cried since his father died.

When he could bear to turn and look again, he noticed the other houses. Deacon Loring's and Joshua Bond's, their neighbors' homes, were also burning. Dark smoke filled the sky above the three houses, and Nathaniel could hear the crackling of wood as they were all consumed by the fire.

It was obvious he wasn't going to get the hidden ammunition that he hoped to find behind the clock shop. He decided to work his way back toward the center of town, rejoin John and the Lexington men he could find, and possibly share some of their ammunition. He was determined to stay with the Regulars when they moved, all the way to Boston if possible, and harass the troops in any way he could; he now had a score to settle!

Chapter 15

April 19, 1775
Late afternoon

Samuel finally reached Lexington Green well after the reinforcements had rescued the straggling column that had marched out the night before. He couldn't get past the eastern edge of the Green as the road was still guarded by the Regulars; he was stunned to see the damage to the meetinghouse. Samuel turned toward Buckman Tavern, hoping to find Nathaniel or John. He didn't have to go far. As soon as he turned Duchess toward the left, he heard someone call his name.

"Samuel! Samuel!" It was Nathaniel, standing on the far edge of the Green, just across from Buckman's. "Thank God you're safe!"

"Looks like this has been a terrible day here, Nathaniel. What happened?"

"We had gathered our men on the Green, simply to show our determination to protect our town. Our lines did not block the road that the Regulars were taking, but they attacked us while we stood there. Seven of our men died, as well as a man from Woburn who had been seized while the Regulars marched from Boston. Another ten men were wounded."

"Dear Lord, that's horrible," Samuel said.

"But we ambushed them on their return from Concord, and it looks like many other towns have sent men to join in. To make matters worse, our house and two others were torched and have been destroyed."

"Where's your family? Were they able to get out before the house was burned down?" a worried Samuel asked.

"We had a plan to get them out if the Regulars came through town. My brother, Sam, took all of them to a farm known by one of our men, Elijah Sanderson, located in the Woburn/Billerica area. They'll stay there until we tell them it is safe, but I don't know where they'll go when they return."

"What are your next steps? Will you be staying in town?"

Nathaniel shook his head. "No. We've been ordered to wait here until the army starts to move. They're holding the road toward Boston, treating their wounded at Munroe Tavern. Eventually, as they move out, we'll follow. Many men from other communities continue to come into town and can help us chase them back to the city."

"We must all stick together. How can I help?" Samuel asked.

"Dr. Fiske, our town doctor, is in Buckman's. He may need your assistance."

Nathaniel and Samuel went toward Buckman Tavern, meeting John as they got to the front door.

"Samuel, so glad to see you are safe. We've had so much tragedy here since you left."

"I know. Nathaniel filled me in. Let's see what needs to be done."

Dr. Joseph Fiske was inside the tavern, discussing with Captain Parker the serious wounds that the Lexington men had suffered. Some of the most seriously hurt were taken to homes nearby while those with less serious wounds still planned to follow the soldiers out of town. Sporadic shooting continued outside as the militia fired at the outer edges of the Regular forces.

Dr. Fiske was glad to see Samuel. He asked, "Can you stay here to assist me?"

"Of course," Samuel replied. "Are there any men who need my attention at this moment?"

"No. But we may need to examine six of the Regulars who've been moved into a back room."

"I'm at your disposal, sir," Samuel responded. "I'm sorry for your niece Ruth's loss this morning. I know she and Jonathan mean a lot to you."

CHAPTER 15

"Thanks, Samuel. Been a tough day for many people in town. I will let you know what help we need. Just stay nearby for now." He left to go to the rear of the tavern to check on the wounded Regulars.

As long as Samuel knew Lydia was out of danger, he would help wherever needed. He joined Nathaniel and John, who were talking with Elijah Sanderson.

"Elijah, this is Dr. Samuel Prescott, Lydia's fiancée," Nathaniel said. "Elijah is a member of our militia group, Samuel. He has been courting our sister, Mary, for a while now and helped us plan what to do with our family if the Regulars came through town."

"Yes, I met Dr. Prescott once or twice at Sunday services in the past. Sorry to see you again under such tragic conditions, Doctor."

"Call me Samuel. Nice to see you again, Elijah."

Discussions began about getting additional food and supplies to the Mullikens since they had only taken enough for a day. The family had no place to return to, with the house now gone, and what they had taken with them wasn't sufficient. After the houses had been set ablaze, people in the village started gathering supplies to help the families affected. Many of the women in town had been consoling friends who had lost husbands, fathers, brothers, or sons in the battle that morning and wanted to do more. Word spread quickly of the need for the Mulliken, Loring, and Bond families. Anna Munroe, whose husband owned Munroe Tavern, being used now as a field hospital by the Regulars, coordinated the effort with other women in town. Ruth Buckman and her husband, John, who owned Buckman Tavern, made space at their tavern for goods that were gathered. Pastor Clarke's wife, Elizabeth, sent out messengers to other homes outside town to bring any extra blankets, clothing, or food to the tavern. Sarah Childs, who frequently sat with Mrs. Mulliken at Sunday services and was pregnant with her sixth child, had her other children gather any unused items at their house and delivered them to the tavern.

Elijah offered to take whatever was collected to the Mullikens first thing in the morning.

Nathaniel told him, "I don't want to put this burden on you, my friend, but you'll have to let my mother know about the house."

"Anything you need, Nathaniel. You, John, and your family have always been so kind to me."

"And getting a chance to see my sister, Mary, won't hurt, right?" said John.

Elijah blushed and repeated, "I'll do whatever you need."

"Can I ask a special favor, Elijah?" Samuel asked. "Can you take a note from me to Lydia? I just want her to know I'm safe and thinking of her."

Nathaniel smacked his hand on the table. "Oh, Samuel. I'm so sorry. With all of this going on, I never thought of that." He called to the owner of the tavern, "John, do you have any paper and a pen for my friend?"

John Buckman left the taproom, went into the kitchen where he had a small desk for his bookkeeping, and brought out some paper and a quill pen and ink for Samuel.

"You know, Dr. Prescott, Parliament expects me to tax you for that document," John said sarcastically. "But we'll let it go this time."

Samuel sat at one of the tables, dipped the quill pen into the ink bottle, and wrote a message for Lydia.

My dearest Lydia,

When I left you last night, feeling such happiness from our time together, I didn't know or expect that today would bring such chaos to our lives. I'm fine, and I wanted you to know I am safe. Nathaniel and John are also safe; we're together now. I promise when things settle down and this all passes, I'll find you, wherever you are, so we can once again be together. I long to look into your eyes and see your beautiful smile. God be with you and your family.

Until I hold you in my arms again,
Your adoring Samuel

CHAPTER 15

Samuel blew onto the letter to help the ink dry, wiping some ink that dripped onto his leg. He slowly rolled the paper, reached into his pocket, and took out the lavender ribbon she had given him for luck. He tied it around the roll of paper and gave it to Elijah.

"Please make sure she gets this, Elijah." Samuel said.

Elijah nodded. "I'll be heading out first thing in the morning, Samuel. You have my word."

As they finished speaking, Nathan Munroe came barging through the door. "They have started marching!" he yelled.

Captain Parker ordered his men to grab their weapons and cartridge boxes and head toward the retreating army. "Follow them from a distance. Try to stay abreast of them along the way, and pick your shots. Remember, they have many more men than when they came this morning, and many are fresh and rested. Be careful of any flankers sweeping the sides of the road as they march. Good luck!"

Samuel watched as Nathaniel and John joined the men and headed out. Nathaniel tipped his hat as he left, gave Samuel a slight grin, and turned and headed across the Green.

Dr. Fiske called out to Samuel, "Stay behind the militia lines as they move forward. We'll need to be ready to provide care to any of the men hit by return fire."

"Yes, Doctor. I'm ready to help where needed."

The doctors grabbed their bags, mounted their horses, and followed behind the Lexington men as they pursued the Regulars out of town.

Nathaniel and John followed the column of soldiers as it struggled to get back to the safety of the city. Swarms of minutemen from surrounding towns continued to swell on both sides of the road ahead, in pursuit of the troops. The Regulars were now being funneled through a gauntlet of musket fire.

Nathaniel checked his cartridge box and realized his ammunition was dwindling with each careful shot. He would crouch behind rail fences and stone walls along the way, pick a target and fire, then run back into the woods to reload. Sometimes he would fire from behind a large oak or around the corner of a building, but he and John slowly and carefully made their way through Menotomy, doing their best to avoid the occasional flankers sent out to protect the column.

At one section of the road that turned to the left, John went behind a house as Nathaniel ran across the field beside it. His right foot stepped into a hole, and he fell forward, losing his musket and tumbling to the ground. As he reached for his gun and tried to stand, he heard someone behind him.

"Damn rebel!" It was one of the flankers, raising his musket to shoot at Nathaniel.

Somehow, the gun misfired. The soldier turned it around and used the butt end to hit Nathaniel, striking him on the side of the head and knocking him down again. As Nathaniel turned, he saw the soldier ready to lunge at him with his bayonet when a shot rang out, striking the soldier and killing him. John had stopped to check on his brother and had come around the house just as the soldier was preparing to use the bayonet on Nathaniel.

"That was close." A relieved Nathaniel sighed. "Nice shot, John. Thank you."

"We have to be careful of those flankers. Let's keep going," John said, reloading his musket.

Nathaniel was still shaking from the encounter but looked at the dead soldier and saw his cartridge box. He opened the cover and saw it was half full, so he quickly grabbed some cartridges and added them to his almost depleted supply.

"Let's use some of the king's ammunition on his own army," he said with a wink to John.

They rejoined the continual flow of men as the road continued closer to Boston. It was getting near dusk, which meant the battle that day was near an end, but they all knew it was from over.

Within the train of wounded, tired, and constantly harassed soldiers retreating for safety in the city, Major Pitcairn did his best to keep rallying his men to fight back and keep the militiamen at bay. Occasionally, one of the cannons that had rescued them was deployed to fire at the groups following them, dispersing them and giving the rear of the Regulars some relief. Battles were fought within private homes and in taverns along the roads through Menotomy

CHAPTER 15

and Cambridge until, at last, as darkness approached, the Regulars reached a safe haven in Charlestown. The exhausted soldiers collapsed as the nightmare of the day finally ended. A day that had different expectations ended with both sides seeing the events in opposite perspectives.

CHAPTER 16

April 20, 1775
Morning

How do you tell someone their family home is gone? Elijah Sanderson wondered, repeating that question in his mind as he rode out of Lexington toward the Latham's farm. He had a wagon full of supplies, food, and clothing from the people in town. He was excited to see Mary again but dreaded breaking the news about the house to her family.

At the Latham's farm, Sam was getting the horses and wagon ready for the trip home they were all expecting. The Latham house was full of activity as Myles filled the fireplace and Prudence prepared breakfast for everyone. A cauldron of baked beans was simmering in the fireplace for supper later, with the sweet aroma of molasses floating throughout the house. Lydia, Mary, and their mother put the bedrooms back together as the two youngest were outside, visiting Rufus and Erasmus.

Elijah rode up to the farm, tying his horse to the rail fence in front and removing the backboards of the wagon. He waved to Sam, who was near the barn, then headed up the short walkway toward the house. Mary came running out when she heard the wagon approaching and saw Elijah.

"Elijah, I'm so glad to see you," she said.

"Mary, I have some terrible news. Your…"

"My brothers? Oh no, what happened?"

CHAPTER 16

"No, your brothers are fine, at least they were when I left them last night. But the Regulars burned down your house and the clock shop, as well as the homes of the Bonds and Lorings."

Mary put her hand to her mouth. Behind her, as the others came outside, Mary heard her mother gasp. Myles followed shortly behind.

"I'm so sorry to bring such bad news, Mrs. Mulliken. Nathaniel and John wanted you to know, and I had offered to bring these items since they knew you only had enough for a day. Many of the families in town brought extra clothing and goods when they knew I was coming."

"Thank you, Elijah," Lydia said as she put her arm around her mother to comfort her.

Sam pulled up with the horses and wagon, thinking they were preparing to leave for home.

"Sam, the Regulars burned our house down," his mother told him.

"Those scum!" he shouted. "I hope Nathaniel and John kill them all."

"What are we going to do now?" Mrs. Mulliken asked Sam and Lydia. "We only took what we thought we needed to get through yesterday."

Myles was shaking his head in disgust. He paced up and down the side of the road, stroking his beard in thought. "I might have an answer. Maybe I can help," he finally said. "There is a former business partner of mine, Ashton Bagley, who lives between here and Boston, in Medford. The fool is a passionate Tory and supporter of the Crown. But he's also a coward. Once he heard about the events yesterday in Lexington and Concord, he and his wife may have abandoned their home to go into Boston for protection, and likely look for the next ship back to London. Sam, let's take your wagon and see what we can find out. Maybe if they're gone, you can use their house until you find something permanent."

The big man rattled the wagon as he climbed aboard next to Sam. Sam urged the horses to get them moving, and they disappeared slowly down the road.

Everyone else went back inside, except Elijah who unpacked the food, supplies, and clothing he had brought. When he went inside,

Lydia asked if he had heard any news about what had happened when the Regulars reached Concord.

"Oh Lydia, I completely forgot. I have something for you." He reached into his jacket pocket and took out the note from Dr. Prescott, still tied with the lavender ribbon.

Lydia was surprised to see the lavender ribbon that she had given Samuel and the note. She collapsed onto a chair and very gingerly untied the ribbon, her hands trembling, unrolled the letter, and read it to herself. Her face relaxed, and she sighed once she read that he was safe.

She looked up at Elijah. "Do you know where he is now?"

"I believe he was helping Dr. Fiske, following the militia as they pursued the soldiers back to Boston. He wanted to be able to help treat the wounded along the way. By nightfall, they probably reached the outskirts of the city. He's most likely with the militia if they set up camp there."

Lydia reached up and removed a white ribbon from her hair and replaced it with the lavender one that she had given Samuel for luck.

When Lydia stood up, her mother was standing in the center of the room, wringing her hands, but standing defiantly. "So, so much has happened the past couple of days, but we must stay together and be strong. As long as each of you is safe, we'll deal with all of this together."

Lydia and Mary hugged their mother as Elijah and Prudence went back to unpacking his delivery. Together, the women started the evening meal, waiting for the return of Sam and Myles. As the sun started to drop toward the horizon, the rich fragrance of a turkey roasting and apple cider brewing in a pot over the fireplace filled the Latham house.

As Prudence and Mrs. Mulliken prepared the table, Joseph jumped up from his spot on the floor and ran outside, yelling to all as he went, "I think I hear them coming!"

In the distance, the creaking of the old wagon was occasionally punctuated with a muffled "Hah!" Yes, it was Myles and Sam returning from their exploratory trip to Medford. Everyone ran outside to welcome them back and see what they had found out.

CHAPTER 16

Myles looked giddy as they reached his house. "I may not enjoy anything today as much as the news I have for you, Mulliken family! Yes, just as I expected, the Bagleys panicked and fled back to military protection in Boston—and are probably waiting for a ship to London in the morning. Looks like they took their clothes, some valuables and their horses, but everything else is there for you—food, bedding, firewood."

Sam added, "It's almost the size of our house, with room for everyone. It will do fine if we borrow it until we can find a place back in Lexington."

"Are you sure this is all right, Myles? That's their home," Mrs. Mulliken asked.

Myles smiled at her and replied, "I assure you they are long gone. Once an outbreak of violence like yesterday happened, Ashton knew that he was such an outspoken Loyalist he would have risked being tarred and feathered if he stayed. And if someone doesn't like it, they can take it up with me!" He raised his arms and tried to look tough and mean, with a scowl on his face.

"Hah!" said Joseph, pointing at the large man. Myles's eyes opened wide in surprise at that reaction, and everyone laughed.

Myles patted Joseph on the top of his head, hugged his wife, and smiled at Lydia. "I hope this softens some of the bad news you've all received lately."

"Yes, Mr. Latham. Thank you so much," she answered.

They helped Myles and Sam pack up the extra supplies and clothing that Elijah had brought earlier while dinner finished cooking. Then they all enjoyed their last meal with their wonderful hosts. After dinner and before darkness settled in, the Mullikens headed to their new place of shelter. It was a red saltbox with a black door. There was a split rail fence running along both sides of the property, and a stone wall lined the edge of the roadway. With three bedrooms upstairs, a kitchen and main room on the first floor, it was just the right size for the Mullikens for the time being. None of them knew how long they would have to stay or what they would be facing in the days ahead.

Chapter 17

Late May to early June 1775

The first few weeks in the temporary house passed quickly as the Mullikens adjusted to a new home. As May came and the days warmed, gardens were planted, and outside activities increased. Mrs. Mulliken yearned for her well-kept garden at their house in Lexington and knew there were still some plants in the gardens there that she could transplant to the gardens at this new house. One morning, she asked Lydia to go with her to see, for the first time, what was left of their former house. They had stored some of their silver in a stone wall out back, and she wanted to see if it was still there. Myles drove the wagon for them while Sam and Mary stayed with Rebeckah and Joseph.

It was a strange feeling, coming back into Lexington after being gone for almost a month. Not much had changed, except for the renewal of life presented by late spring in flourishing trees and blossoming plants. As they approached their old property and saw the devastation, Mrs. Mulliken put her hand to her mouth. Only the stone fireplace remained standing, with charred timbers and piles of blackened wood where the proud house had once stood. The clock shop was completely gone, with several pieces of metal clockwork mechanisms scattered outside.

Myles helped the two women down from the wagon, and they sifted through the ashes, looking for anything they could salvage. Occasionally, they found a piece of silverware or a pewter mug. Mrs. Mulliken turned over a charred pot that was on the floor near the

CHAPTER 17

fireplace and found a partial cover of *Pilgrim's Progress*, protected from the fire by the metal pot. A large piece of the spinning wheel laid charred nearby. Lydia went to the stone wall in back, rolled down a large stone, and found a bag of some of the valuables they had hidden before leaving. She gave them to Myles to load into the wagon.

Afterward, Myles went to the gardens to dig up some lavender plants, sage, and thyme as chosen by Mrs. Mulliken, as well as her favorite bergamot used for Oswego tea. Meanwhile, Lydia thought of her place of solitude on the slope overlooking the town; the place she had shared the last moments with Samuel. She walked up the small hill and sat on the large rock, looking down on the town. Their lives had been turned upside down after that dreadful April day, but after all that the village had also suffered through, most of Lexington looked unchanged. Lydia started to return to her mother's side, stopping to reach up and remove the new ribbon she was wearing in her hair. She turned to a small tree on the walkway back to the house and tied the ribbon to a branch. *Maybe he will come by here one day*, she thought to herself.

Little did she know, Samuel would be there sooner than she imagined.

When Lydia returned to the house, Myles was helping her mother back into the wagon. He had loaded the few things they were able to find that were salvageable and was waiting for Lydia. They headed back to Medford with what they had found, and as they pulled away, Mrs. Mulliken looked back, sadness reflected on her face, with so many memories in what was now ruins. Lydia put her arm around her mother to comfort her. Myles glanced back at them, a tear in his eye, as quiet as he had ever been.

Outside of Boston, the troops had received welcome news that the colonials, led by Ethan Allen and Benedict Arnold, had captured Fort Ticonderoga in New York. It gave them some hope as the siege outside the city had started to drain resources. Samuel continued to work with Dr. Fiske and other physicians who were part of the local militias, supported and encouraged by visits and assistance from Doctor Warren. They were busy helping those still recovering from wounds received during the pursuit of the Regulars returning from

Concord, as well as the occasional excursions the troops had tried to make from the city, looking for supplies. Amputations, broken-bone repair, hunger and dehydration were too common. Some illnesses had also started spreading as the camps grew, circling the city from Roxbury to Chelsea. Supplies for the medical needs were diminishing, causing some concern among the doctors. Dr. Prescott was certain there might be additional supplies back home, as his father typically kept a substantial stock of items for himself and his sons for their patients' needs. He requested permission to ride home and see what he could gather and was told to make the trip and return the same day.

Samuel mounted Duchess and headed west. As he entered Lexington, he knew he would have to pass by the remnants of the Mullikens' house. He had not seen it since the day it was burned down, having passed while it was still smoldering when he was leaving town that fateful day, following the militia troops toward the city. This was his first opportunity to really examine what was there.

Samuel stopped on the side of the road and trembled at the sight of the devastation. He walked over to where the front door had been—where he had said goodbye that night—and crouched, the anguish and pain gripping him. He picked up a piece of charred wood, imagining it as likely a piece of the door as it had hinges on one small section. He was so relieved that Lydia and her family had been able to get away before it had been torched by the Regulars. He remembered what a nice supper they had shared that night, his conversations with Nathaniel, and his walk with Lydia.

Suddenly, it dawned on him—the walk they took was a short distance from the house, and he could go back, helping to relive the memories from that night. Samuel headed up the small slope and was happy when he found the large rock that they had rested on at the top. The view of Lexington was different during the day, and the stars they had admired weren't visible in the bright daylight. He sat there, quietly reflecting on how he had felt that night. And then he saw it, slowly fluttering in the breeze as if it was waving to him—a ribbon tied to a branch. Samuel jumped up and grabbed it, holding it and examining it. The ribbon appeared almost new, so he

CHAPTER 17

realized—stunned—that she must have put it there only a short time ago. How deeply disappointed Samuel felt, knowing he might have seen her if he had been there earlier.

Samuel realized she might come back at some point, so he carefully tied it around the trunk of the same tree, easy for her to see. He hoped she would come back at some point and see it, knowing he had found her "message."

He returned to Duchess and turned her toward Concord. Arriving at his house, his mother and Lucy screamed with delight when Samuel walked in the door, hugging him so much he couldn't breathe. He was pleased that his father and Benjamin were home. Samuel was relieved that Abel Jr. was resting comfortably in his room, still recovering from that wound in his side. Several infections had made it more difficult to overcome, but Abel was still his positive, happy self and very glad to see Samuel.

"My dear brother, what a joy seeing you here," he said as Samuel walked into the room. "I'm so glad you are safe. What brings you here?"

"Abel, it's such a difficult time. I wish you were with me through this, by my side. I could really use your help. So many injuries and disease to deal with every day. And we're all struggling to keep up with the need for supplies. I was hoping Father would have some here that he might be able to spare."

His father was standing at the door and overheard him. "Of course, Samuel. We've been stocking up with what we need in the event the conflict came back into the countryside. There are no supplies coming through Boston, but we've been able to move items through Portsmouth and Providence."

Benjamin joined him. "And fortunately, some of the ships coming from England with supplies for the army have been intercepted, providing us with another resource. What do you need in particular?"

"Cloth for wrapping wounds, splints, leather strips, any camphor, cinchona bark, or other medications," answered Samuel. "But I don't want to leave you short."

His father shook his head. "Don't worry about that, Samuel. Dr. Minot also has sufficient supplies stored in Liberty Tavern, if needed."

Samuel and Benjamin loaded the items that were available into a large canvas bag. The family shared a meal together, but Samuel took his plate and went to sit with Abel in his room. He wanted to spend some time with his brother.

As the early evening started to fade into darkness, Samuel draped the canvas bag with supplies over Duchess. He stood at the door to say goodbye.

"Please take care of yourself, son," his father said, putting his right hand behind Samuel's neck.

"I will, Father. Thank you for your help."

Samuel's mother looked at him with tears in her eyes. "I'm so afraid I'll never see you again. Come back whenever you get the chance, just to calm my fears," she asked him.

"I'm sure I'll find some time to visit, Mother. There is just so much going on right now, but hopefully, it will quiet down in time."

Both Lucy and Benjamin gave him a hug, and as he turned, he realized he hadn't said goodbye to Abel. He went into the house to see his brother while the rest of the family stood, waiting for him.

"On your way back?" Abel asked.

"Yes, but I couldn't leave without saying goodbye. I wish you were well enough to come with me. I could use your guidance and support, but please rest and get well." Samuel stroked his brother's right arm as he stood next to the bed.

"One of these days we can get back to Wright's and finish our conversations with the others," Abel said. "In the meantime, take good care of our men. We need them healthy to ensure the Regulars don't return to Concord and hurt other people."

Samuel nodded and went to the door. He turned to take one last look at his brother. Abel grimaced but smiled at him as Samuel headed outside.

Climbing into his saddle, Samuel waved to his parents and siblings, turned Duchess, and headed back toward Cambridge, pausing for a brief moment as he again passed the ashes of the once happy Mulliken house.

Chapter 18

June 12–16, 1775

The tension and anger in Boston were reaching a boiling point. Because of the siege that surrounded the city, food and supplies were getting scarce. Farmers who had been accustomed to bringing their goods into the city from their local farms now had difficulty getting into Boston. The Loyalists in town were pointing fingers of blame at those who supported the colonists for the current problems. The army was not receiving its normal supplies from England, as some of the ships were lost at sea or intercepted, with important items being taken for use by the rebellion instead. The livestock normally found in nearby farms was now being sent from overseas but often didn't survive the trip. After receiving one such shipment, General Gage expressed his frustration to Major Pitcairn.

"John, this is getting ridiculous. Look at this manifest from yesterday: 550 sheep ordered, only 40 received; 290 hogs requested, 74 made it alive. Hundreds of barrels of flour arrived rancid. Only half the ships made it into port because of gales and pirates."

"Yes, General, it has been difficult. Many of the townspeople are rumbling, even many Loyalists. Most are even more upset because of the arrival of our four thousand reinforcements. The loyal people are wondering how we're going to feed all of the additional forces. The people in town are looking for some type of military action to free the city of the siege," replied the major.

"We're fortunate to also have the arrival of Major General William Howe and Brigadier Generals Henry Clinton and John

Burgoyne to help guide us through this. We'll all meet tomorrow to plan some movement to gain some relief." General Gage threw the manifest on his desk, disgusted. "I've even sent my wife back to London, fearful for her safety but also to keep all details of our plans as secret as possible."

Major Pitcairn bowed and said, "I shall see you in the morning, sir. I look forward to reviewing your plans with the generals."

The commanding officers of the Royal Army met the next day at Province House to finalize details of an assault to break the siege. General Gage sat at his desk while Howe, Burgoyne, and Clinton sat in front of him, Lord Percy standing to his left. Major Pitcairn sat further away, in a chair next to the window. The preliminary plan they were discussing involved one group of troops crossing Boston Neck and attacking the southern section of the semicircle of camps in Roxbury. Another larger group would cross Charlestown Neck and try to divide the remaining militia camps then sweep southward, destroying the siege.

The discussion became very animated between the officers who had been stationed in Boston for a while and the new officers who had just arrived. General John Burgoyne, in particular, was flabbergasted that the Regulars were somehow being held "hostage" in the city.

"Gage, you're telling me that only ten to twelve thousand farmers and shopkeepers are intimidating more than six thousand brave, strong royal troops? We've fought and defeated larger, more skilled, and tougher armies than those rebels." He shook his head in obvious disgust.

"And we have the ships' cannons and far more firepower that hasn't even been used," added General William Howe.

"I understand your concerns, gentlemen," replied General Gage. "But these rebels have more skill, more determination, and more discipline than you realize. Many of their officers were veterans of our army and have fought on this continent for years. Ask Pitcairn—he saw it firsthand on our first attempt to disarm the rebels." Gage gestured to the major, waving his arm.

CHAPTER 18

Major Pitcairn ran his right hand through his thinning hair, took a deep breath, and stood to address the generals. "I understand the frustration felt by my superiors, and yes, General Gage, I did see a more tenacious and engaged group of fighters in April. But it was on their terms and on their turf. At the time, even though they were undisciplined, they had the protection of fighting from behind fences, walls and buildings, as well as knowing the area better than our troops. I still strongly believe, taking the fight directly to them with a major assault would send them running like scared dogs."

General Gage looked at the determined faces of the other officers, nodded at Major Pitcairn, and told them to finish developing the plans then decide which companies would be used. He ordered them to give him final details the next day. He wanted the assault to be launched on Sunday, June 18. Gage's final instructions were for the troops to be provided with three days' provisions, so once they captured the peninsula leading out of Charlestown and started to circle through the rebel camps, they would be sufficiently supplied.

In Philadelphia, the Second Continental Congress had assembled in May, continuing its discussions on demanding freedom and rights. With the conflict that had started in Lexington and Concord and the ongoing siege of Boston, it wanted a central commander to organize and direct the militias. On June 14, it chose George Washington of Virginia to be commander in chief of the newly formed Continental Army; it also approved the commission of major general for Dr. Joseph Warren, based on his continued leadership and planning skills throughout the siege. This commission was dispatched to be delivered to Dr. Warren as soon as possible.

Back in Cambridge, the provincials were also making plans. Samuel and Dr. Fisk were summoned to Hastings House for a council of officers and a few of the small number of doctors. They were introduced to some new officers who had been working with other troops along the siege line. First, there was Henry Knox, the former bookstore owner, who had fled the city after the Lexington and Concord encounters, fearing for his life. His bookstore had been ransacked, burned, and looted after his departure. His wife, Lucy, was estranged from a very Loyalist family, so he was glad to be out of

Boston. Also joining the forces was Israel Putnam from Connecticut, who explained that he had left his plow in the field immediately upon hearing of actions in Concord and had come there ready to help, but arrived unarmed. One of the commanders, Artemas Ward, called over one of the officers in the camp with a gift for Putnam—the silver pistols that had been lost by Major Pitcairn on the retreat from Concord. The council was meeting to discuss plans going forward and improving fortifications in the event General Gage and his officers decided to go on the offensive. The officers were concerned that the Royal Army would attack in an effort to dislodge or break up the forces of local militia surrounding the city. Because of his many contacts within Boston, Dr. Joseph Warren had worked with the officers for many days to create the best strategy to provide protection from such an attack.

Later that week, as the final rays of the sun set over the trees behind him on a quiet Friday night, Samuel slowly walked to the shoreline of the Charles River, another long, grueling, and emotionally draining day finally coming to a close. Here it was, mid-June, and he continued to deal with helping those militia members who were still recovering from the wounds they had received pursuing the Regulars back from Concord and Lexington. Some were fighting infections, some needed amputations and subsequent recovery, and there was a growing concern of smallpox spreading. Inoculations for that dreaded disease were not yet an option; the men with high fevers, body aches, severe stomach pain and rashes—symptoms of the disease—were quarantined as soon as possible to help reduce spread.

Samuel sat down to rest on an old log, looking across the mouth of the river at Boston, seeing a few glimmering lanterns in the windows of homes and shops. The dark, haunting shadows of a few warships lurked on the waves in the harbor, their tall masts silhouetted against the darkening sky. Glancing to his left, Samuel could see in the distance the steeple of a church rising above a nearly vacant Charlestown, looking ghostly in the evening mist that was hanging over the water. The sight of the church made him think of his friend, Reverend William Emerson, who had made several trips to Cambridge to offer his meetinghouse and even his own home to

CHAPTER 18

Harvard College since the campus was being used for new recruit training. He always found Samuel to offer some friendship and encouragement, and his visits always lifted Samuel's spirits. Now, sitting there in the dark, Samuel felt much anguish, overwhelmed by the needs of the men in his care and the desperation of trying to make supplies last. He couldn't shake a sense of impending doom and sat alone, his head bowed in his hands, taking long deep breaths. Despite his knowledge and skill, the exhaustion and stress were taking a toll on him. He looked down at his hands, which he had always treasured as steady, strong instruments to help people, but they were shaking. He wished so much he could see Lydia, or at least have his brother, Abel, working alongside him as support.

But Samuel also knew he needed to be strong for the other doctors and for his patients, who had put their life on the line for the common cause. There was no time for self-pity, worrying about his own struggles. There was work to be done, patients who needed his care. He slowly stood, took one more deep breath, and started back to camp, so preoccupied with his thoughts he never looked up at the stars—something he had become accustomed to doing for comfort since that night with Lydia. His duty once again called.

As Samuel made his way back to camp, he passed several groups of men heading toward Charlestown Neck with shovels and picks. He thought it looked peculiar at this time of night and asked one of the men where they were going.

"We have orders to report to Bunker Hill," one of the men responded. "We have some work to do to make it more defensible. We believe an assault by the Regulars is imminent."

Samuel nodded, even though he didn't always understand military decisions, and returned to camp. He was met by Dr. Fiske, who asked him to pack some items he would need for a field hospital that was being set up early the next morning on the Cambridge side of Charlestown Neck. Samuel gathered what he thought would be necessary. After preparing his supplies, he tried to get some rest. He fell asleep, thinking of Lydia and also wishing there was more he could do personally to help these men who had such passion for their cause.

CHAPTER 19

June 16–17, 1775

Once the true plans of the Royal Army were discovered by spies in Boston and relayed to Dr. Warren, the colonial officers knew they had to act. Word of a potential attack hastened their planning. To make the first move, plans were developed to fortify one of the hills overlooking Boston on the peninsula on Charlestown Neck. The original plan was for Bunker Hill, taller of the two main hills, but the officers in charge of the plan and the men who volunteered mistakenly went farther, to the hill closest to the harbor, Breed's Hill. About a thousand men, including Nathaniel and John Mulliken, marched in the early darkness of June 16, working as quietly as possible. The colonial forces used shovels and picks to dig up soil, dirt, and stones and built a square earthen wall, 6 feet high and about 130 feet across, creating a barricade overlooking the ships in the harbor. Sticks, branches, and sections of fence were mixed into the wall to provide some extra protection. The soil they removed to build the walls created an effective defensive ditch in front.

Looking out over the newly constructed walls as they grew larger, Nathaniel pointed out to John the candles flickering in the city's windows, but even more ominous were those on the decks of the ships just off the bottom of the gentle slope falling to the sea below them. As they spoke quietly, one of the commanding officers, Colonel William Prescott, joined the work; he had come with his Pepperell and Groton men and stopped to check on their progress.

CHAPTER 19

"Colonel Prescott, are you related to the Concord Prescotts?" Nathaniel whispered as he shoveled more dirt onto the wall.

"Not that I am aware of," replied the colonel. "Family friends?"

"Yes, sir," answered Nathaniel before turning to move a large stone.

Soon after, the brothers were surprised to see the arrival of Dr. Joseph Warren, as he came to join in the work and prepare for a potential fight.

"Nathaniel and John, so good to see you. Been an interesting couple of months since you delivered my clock," he said, smiling. They both nodded as they continued the laborious task, stopping only briefly to strike up conversations with the men near them.

"Are you fellows from Colonel Prescott's company?" John asked several other men as they rolled a log onto the wall.

"Some of us are," answered one man. "I'm Ebenezer Bancroft of Dunstable. This is Benjamin Ward, and over there is Wainwright Fisk, brave Pepperell patriots," he said, pointing to two men near him.

"And I am Amos Farnsworth of Groton," said a man on the other side of Nathaniel.

A black man, one of several, on the other side of the Pepperell men stopped shoveling for a moment, wiping his brow. "Nice to meet you, gentlemen. I'm Peter Salem, from Framingham. My friend here is Caesar Bason, and over there is Prince Hall. It's a pleasure working with all of you."

They all smiled and nodded, getting back to work. The officers were trying to get some water, or at least some rum, to help quench the thirst from the dusty conditions and grueling work.

Another man mentioned he had come from Dunstable with Captain Bancroft, but in his attempt to stay very quiet, Nathaniel could not hear his name. "We marched down just this week," he heard him tell another man. "Asa Kendall, our local tavernkeeper, has supplies stored in his attic and provided us with cartridges and powder."

"It's a good thing he did," added Colonel Prescott. "We're very limited in how much ammunition we have. Each of you will be given fifteen rounds in addition to what you had on your own."

As the night wore on, Nathaniel stopped momentarily to look at the men from so many different towns, as well as New Hampshire and Connecticut, who had come to help. When the height of the walls neared completion, Dr. Warren noticed it would be difficult to fire over the six-foot-high walls and suggested some type of firing platform for the men to stand on. Unfortunately, there weren't many carpenters in the group.

Some of the men volunteered to build something, and Dr. Warren said to Nathaniel, "You and your brother are expert clockmakers. Surely you can assist?"

"Not our specialty, but we'll come up with something," Nathaniel replied.

Colonel Prescott sent two Lunenburg men, Thomas Wetherbee and William Wyman, to get some planks that had been stored on Bunker Hill. The men all worked together to add places to stand so their muskets could be positioned resting on the top of the walls, making it easier to see targets and fire.

Before the sun started to show signs of dawn on the horizon, John, Nathaniel, and the other men stopped to look at their yeoman work. They smiled, nodded at each other, and patted each other on the back, admiring all they had accomplished overnight. However, with morning approaching, the danger and serious nature of why it was done soon created a very somber mood among the participants. Dr. Warren sensed it and walked among the men, offering encouragement and praising their work.

"Nice job, fellows. What a surprise General Gage will have when he sits down for breakfast this morning!" It helped lighten the mood and eased the tension.

CHAPTER 20

June 17, 1775

In the early morning of June 17, General Gage was awakened by one of his aides.

"General, come quickly. Something has happened overnight," the man shouted.

The general went outside, was handed a spyglass by one of several officers who had assembled, and looked in amazement at what appeared to be a fort that had grown out of nowhere on the Charlestown Neck hills in front of him.

"Damn," he said, handing the spyglass to Major Pitcairn who joined him. "Look what they have done overnight. I want several of the ships turned to face that hill and pummel it with cannon fire," he commanded.

The major looked at the barricade and shook his head in disgust. "We must get them out of there, General. It creates a dangerous situation for us, as the rebels getting the high ground could leave us defenseless."

For the next couple of hours, the cannons of the *HMS Lively* pounded the hill, but the earthen wall stood strong. Many of the cannonballs whistled over the heads of the men in the fortifications. Those militiamen who had not experienced any of the fighting during the retreat from Concord and Lexington were getting their first taste of what was to come. The barrage was so fearsome some of them grabbed their muskets and left, but most were prepared to stay and fight. Some were sent to the edges of Charlestown to get water from wells to refresh those who had been there all night but were stunned when Asa Pollard, one of the Billerica men, was beheaded by a cannon ball. It made the whole situation even more tense.

In Boston General Gage gathered the other generals and senior officers to plan a major attack to dislodge the militia from the fortifications. They altered the original plan to cross over Boston Neck to attack the camps in Roxbury and decided a frontal assault on the Charlestown peninsula was necessary. General William Howe would lead a charge up the right side of the slope toward the fortification while General Robert Pigot would take his regiment along the left side with Major Pitcairn and his Marines. The major requested that his son, William, be allowed to help command his Marines. Generals Burgoyne and Clinton commanded the battery of cannons on Copps Hill in Boston.

Up behind the walls, the now exhausted men who had been working all night looked down and saw what they would be facing. Twenty-eight longboats and barges carrying troops in their red coats started across from Boston, landing them on the shore at the bottom of the slopes in front of them. Minutes later, two to three long rows of red-and-white images, stretching across the entire area in front of them, slowly started toward their crude fort.

Throughout the morning and into the early afternoon, many spectators gathered on rooftops in Boston and along the shorelines, enthralled by the military spectacle playing out before them. The cloudless cobalt-blue sky, the gently swaying, tall, green grass on the slope and the soft waves sparkling in the June sun on the harbor did not accurately portray the destruction and human suffering about to unfold. When the assault began at three o'clock in the afternoon, the sound of church bells chiming the time just added to the scene.

As had been discussed the night before, Samuel and some of the other doctors were summoned to the camp directly adjacent to the Charlestown Neck and told to prepare for wounded men being brought back from the fortifications once the battle started. A hastily built field hospital would be their base. Samuel was ready to help but very concerned he might know some of the wounded men if they were from Concord and, even more so, worried one of the Mulliken

CHAPTER 20

brothers could be involved. He steadied himself and made sure he had what he needed.

He asked Dr. Fiske, "Will Dr. Warren be joining us?'

Dr. Fiske shook his head. "No, he has volunteered to fight with the men on the hill. He feels we have enough support here and feels he will be needed more among the soldiers."

Samuel understood—Dr. Warren's sense of duty and responsibility was deeply admired and respected by everyone involved.

As the day went on, what they prepared for was exceeded. The few small injuries at the beginning—exhaustion and dehydration from working through the night, some flash burns from misfiring muskets, and the minor wounds—would start getting worse as the day went on. Men were carried into the area on litters, stretched blankets, or just on the shoulders of others.

Over on Breed's Hill, as the assault began, the left side of the Royal Army's line was under constant attack from snipers in the buildings of now nearly empty Charlestown. Rather than send needed troops into the town to clear out the snipers, the command was given to the ships closest to the town to fire red-hot cannonballs and balls filled with burning pitch into the village, starting a roaring fire that eventually consumed the town. A landing crew was sent to add to the burning of the buildings closest to the shore. The tall, majestic steeple that marked the Charlestown skyline was soon engulfed in flames and toppled with a crash. Dark smoke climbing upward added to the scene as the village was soon totally ablaze; there was no more firing from the buildings.

Behind the walls of the earthen fort, Nathaniel and John stood side by side with the men they had spent the night with, working so hard to build this defense. They all waited for orders as the multitude of soldiers in front of them began their assault. General Putnam and Colonel Prescott walked along behind them, shouting encouragement. Dr. Warren stood a few feet from Nathaniel, peering over the wall to watch the advance of the enemy.

Nathaniel turned to his brother, knowing they were in a dangerous situation, and asked, "Are you ready?"

"Oh, definitely," John said. "This is for our friend, Caleb, and the other men who died on the Green the last time we were attacked."

"And for what they did to our house—and to protect our family," answered Nathaniel.

"And for liberty!" shouted Peter Salem, bringing cheers from all nearby.

Colonel Prescott was barking instructions. "Remember, men, we have a limited supply of ammunition. Use what you have when ordered, pick your shots, and fall back when your supply is depleted so someone can fill in behind you. There are men ready to step up."

Dr. Warren reminded them of their shooting skills. "I have seen many of you pick off a rabbit from a distance. Concentrate and aim carefully. If the rich tradition of the British Army holds, there will be many officers leading the assault. Take aim at their fancy uniforms."

General Putnam chimed in, "We will give the order to fire. Be patient. No one is to fire until ordered to do so."

The long, wide line of Regulars moved steadily up the slope through the tall grass, getting closer and closer with each passing moment. John wiped his left hand on his trousers then got a firm grip on the front of his musket. His right cheek pressed against the wood at the butt end of his weapon as he waited.

Even closer the soldiers came, bearing down on them like a rolling wave. Behind him, Nathaniel heard one officer yell, "Don't fire until you see the whites of their eyes. Wait for the order!" He slowly rubbed his finger up and down the trigger, waiting for the command as the oncoming force closed in on them. They could all see every detail of the uniforms of the oncoming enemy.

"Fire! Fire!" came the command at last, and a roar shook the earthen wall as the men lined up behind it let loose a massive volley. Large sections of the front line of soldiers fell, as well as several in the second line. The line halted for an instant, shocked by the barrage; and as they prepared to continue, the colonists had reloaded and fired again. More men went down. Many of the infantry stood and returned fire at the men behind the wall, wounding some of the militia, then the lines turned and retreated, lifting or helping those

CHAPTER 20

who were not as seriously wounded. Men could be heard crying and groaning in the trampled and bloodied grass.

Some of the militiamen were tempted to climb the wall and chase the retreating lines but were kept back by the officers. Many continued to fire but were reminded to save some of their ammunition.

Nathaniel checked on John. "Are you all right?"

"Yes, I'm fine, Nathaniel." He looked over the wall and saw the troops being forced to reform by their officers. "They will be back. How are you set for ammunition?"

"I have another five or six rounds left. Enough to stop them again," Nathaniel said.

In a few minutes, the lines of redcoats were again spread out across the pastures in front of them, starting to gradually work their way back toward the walls of the fort.

The officers behind John and Nathaniel continued to shout orders. "Wait again to fire, men. This time, let them get even closer, and we will hit them even harder!"

Step by step, inch by inch, the line of soldiers came toward them. When the front line of the redcoats reached the area where they had to step over fallen comrades in the grass, the officers in the fort gave the order again. "FIRE!" Almost the entire front line was felled. The men behind the wall reloaded so quickly many of them laid their ramrods by their side rather than return them to their muskets. Firing on both sides was heavy as the redcoats returned fire, and the colonists kept up the intense pace. The soldiers began to turn and retreat again, many running toward the longboats that had transported them to this slaughter. The officers had to stand before them with swords drawn to restore order.

In Boston General Gage had seen the lines begin to retreat again and sent another five hundred soldiers to join the battle. The men at the bottom of the slope now removed their knapsacks, some even their red coats. Heavy artillery fire pounded the fort and adjacent areas while they were reassembled for one more charge. Soon they started back up the hill for another assault.

Behind the wall, many of the men were getting low on ammunition. The officers moved through the fort, checking on each man.

Some of the men shared any extra ammunition, but Nathaniel and John were down to a last cartridge apiece. A few of the men were so desperate for ammunition they used small pebbles that fit into their muskets.

Nathaniel looked at John and told him, "Give me your last round and head back to Bunker Hill for more."

"No way. I'm not leaving you here," his brother shouted. "We came here together and will leave together, one way or another." They grabbed each other's forearms in solidarity and nodded.

Peter Salem wanted a shot at one more officer before he ran out of ammunition. Peering carefully through the clouds of dust and musket smoke as the line came closer, he saw a smartly dressed officer approaching with a large force of soldiers. It was Major John Pitcairn.

Pitcairn had led his Marines up to the front line, which was again being decimated. He shouted over to his son, William, "Lieutenant Pitcairn, have your group form behind my center line. Prepare them to assault the fortification with bayonets."

He then yelled at the line of light infantry struggling in front of him and his Marines. "Break and let us through!" he commanded to many of the soldiers who were starting to fall back a third time. He raised his sword, pointed it at the fort wall in front of them, and shouted, "For the glory of the Marines!"

In the next instant, a musket ball tore into Major Pitcairn's chest. He was thrown back, into the arms of his son, William. The major was quickly carried on his son's shoulders to a boat and transported to army headquarters on Prince Street in Boston, where General Gage had his own doctor examine his wounds, which were considered fatal. He died two hours later, at fifty-two, and was buried in a vault in Old North Church, ironically the same church where the two lanterns illuminated the signal to Paul Revere, starting the ride that intertwined so many of these people and their families.

Inside the fortifications, things were getting desperate. Ammunition was running out as the firing continued, growing in intensity. The endless, deafening sounds of battle surrounded them. Small pebbles and broken nails were being used with the powder poured from broken artillery shells.

CHAPTER 20

As the men finally started running out of ammunition, Colonel Prescott ordered them to start a retreat toward the rear of the fortification and to head for Bunker Hill, where there should be reinforcements to protect them. Dr. Warren organized several men who were fortunate enough to have some ammunition left as well as bayonets and formed a barricade for the men to go through to get out safely. Colonel Prescott fought off the redcoats with his saber as they started to scale the walls and began intense hand to hand combat. As Nathaniel and John passed through the barrier created by Dr. Warren and his group, they asked to stay and fight.

"No, boys, you have done all you can. Your work here is done. We need both of you for the battles yet to come. Go!" Dr. Warren shouted over the roar of the cannons and muskets and the yelling of men on both sides.

Nathaniel and John ran through the wall of men, out the back, and across the field toward Bunker Hill. They were running an endless gauntlet of cannon balls and musket fire, as the redcoats were starting to circle around the back of the fort. Musket balls whistled around them, and cannonballs went over their heads or bounced on the ground and rolled past them. A man a few steps ahead was struck by a musket ball and fell while another man to their left tripped over a fallen comrade. Nathaniel stopped to help him and assisted him to the edge of the field.

"Are you all right?" he asked the fellow fighter.

"Yes, my friend, thank you for your help. I'm Daniel Shays and a truly grateful man."

Together, the three of them struggled successfully to get up to Bunker Hill, where they found most of the men there preparing to withdraw over Charlestown Neck.

Colonel Prescott, his jacket shredded from bayonet attacks, successfully defended himself and some of the remaining men as they retreated from the fort. The swarms of redcoats finally overran the walls and took control of the fort. As the last militiamen made their retreat out the back, Dr. Warren, fighting ferociously to the end, was hit by a musket ball on the side of his head and fell.

In the Cambridge field hospital, it was chaos. The many wounded men, some hurt severely, continued to flood the area. As evening began to envelope them in darkness, the flow of wounded eventually slowed as the battle ended. For some reason, the Royal Forces did not pursue the colonists past Bunker Hill. The doctors in the field hospital did their best to help treat those they could and make them comfortable.

Lieutenant Colonel James Brickett, one of the commanders within the fort but also a doctor, had returned to be treated after getting wounded early in the fight. He told the other doctors of the leadership of Doctor Warren and said he was awaiting Dr. Warren's return to camp to congratulate and thank him.

One of the last wounded men who arrived spoke up. "Did you men not hear? As Dr. Warren bravely protected the final group of men who were retreating, he was hit by musket fire and is believed dead."

A dramatic silence and sadness descended on the area where they were working. It was not the news they had expected.

Similarly, as the last few men retreated across Charlestown Neck, word was passed between them of lost comrades. Prince Hall and Peter Salem told them Caesar Bason did not make it back across the field to Bunker Hill when retreating. Several Pepperell men who had worked alongside the Mulliken brothers were also lost. As the terrible news about Dr. Warren reached Nathaniel, he fell to his knees, devastated.

John stood next to him, squeezing his shoulder. "There was nothing we could have done, Nathaniel." Nathaniel looked up at him, stood, and they embraced.

Although it was a battle that they lost as far as giving up ground, the casualties they had inflicted were double their own. The Royal Army had lost almost one hundred officers as well. The colonists were physically, emotionally, and mentally drained, but it had made them even more determined and more confident that their cause was a just one, worth fighting and dying for. It also exposed their need for more weapons and ammunition, especially artillery.

CHAPTER 20

The day after the battle, General Gage filed a report to Lord Dartmouth, Secretary of State in England, with the casualties and results of the assault. Three days after the report was received in London, Lord Dartmouth issued an order recalling General Gage to England. He was replaced by General William Howe. Gage sailed back to England and never returned to America.

A week after the battle, the militia in camps outside Boston received a great emotional boost with the arrival of General George Washington, bringing his experience and leadership as the siege continued. Also arriving was the major general commission for Doctor Warren, an honor received too late.

Chapter 21

July 1775

News of the defeat on Charlestown Neck circulated throughout Massachusetts and the other colonies. The formation of the Continental Army created an increase in recruiting activities in many of the towns.

One hot and humid July afternoon, while Rebeckah and Joseph were feeding the chickens, Mary went outside to gather some eggs. She saw Sam standing at the end of the stone wall in front of the house, talking to a man she didn't recognize.

When she went back inside, she asked Lydia, "Who is Sam talking to?"

Lydia put down a blanket she was repairing and looked out the front window. She shrugged. "I don't know. He doesn't look familiar to me." She went back to work on the mending.

A few minutes later, Sam came in, carrying a paper with some scribbled writing on it.

Mary asked him, "Who was that man?"

"He's an officer in the new Continental Army. He's recruiting men in this area and stopped to talk to me."

Mrs. Mulliken walked in from a back room while he was talking. "What did he tell you, Sam?"

Sam showed his mother the paper and reviewed the information on it in case she couldn't make out the writing. "As part of building a strong army to fight the Royal Army, well-trained men and supplies are needed. The officer said the Continental Army is looking

CHAPTER 21

for men, sixteen and older, to join. Anyone interested must commit to either one or three years and have the opportunity to reenlist or leave at the end of that time. They will provide a uniform, a musket, ammunition, canteen, and a knapsack. There will be daily food provided—one pound of beef or salt fish, vegetables, rice or corn meal, and milk or cider. And there is a stipend of seven dollars a month."

His mother looked at him to try to read the interest in his face. "Are you considering joining?" she asked.

Sam stared at her for few a few moments then replied, "Yes, Mother. I want to be a part of this fight, like my brothers have been. I can ask Myles to help you around here if you feel it is needed, but Lydia and Mary can do everything that I do. Rebeckah and Joseph are getting older and can also help. But I want your approval."

Mrs. Mulliken handed him the paper and sat in a chair by the fireplace. "I've spent every day and night for the past three months worried sick about your brothers. But after all we've been through since that dreadful day in April, I understand their passion and commitment for this cause. I do not want to see another one of my sons put himself in jeopardy, but will not stand in your way."

Sam knelt in front of her and took her right hand in his hands. "Mother, I don't want to add more worry or stress to what you have been dealing with. But I have the same fight inside me that Nathaniel and John have. I want to show those evil men who did that damage on the Green that we will not sit by and let them take our freedom. They burned down our house. They disrupted our lives. I want to fight to get all of that back. Besides, after father died, Nathaniel was barely older than Joseph is now, and there were seven of us who needed to be cared for. Joseph will be capable of helping you and the three girls while I'm gone."

Lydia and Mary had been standing nearby, stunned by what they heard. They both went to Sam's side. "We'll miss you dearly, Sam," Lydia said. "But we respect your decision."

Mary rubbed his head and told him, "Please be careful. We haven't seen or heard from our brothers but hope they are safe and that you can all be home soon."

Mrs. Mulliken leaned forward and kissed him on the forehead. "When do you have to leave?"

"A group of new enlistees will be passing by here in two days, on the way to Cambridge for recruit training. The officer said he'll watch for me out front. If I'm there, I can join them."

"We'll help you get ready," his mother said. "I'll tell Rebeckah and Joseph tonight. Take the wagon and go tell Myles. Let him know that his help will be welcome and needed."

As darkness fell that night, the family sat together in front of the fireplace after dinner. The news about Sam's future departure had been shared with the two youngest. It was a quiet and somber evening. A soft amber glow from the flickering flames illuminated their worried faces. Mary sat on the floor with her left arm around Joseph; Rebeckah was on a bench next to Sam with her head resting on his right shoulder. Lydia sat in front of her mother who was rocking slowly in her rocking chair.

Mrs. Mulliken spoke softly to her children. "Since your father died, we've had some very dark and sad days. But we've had some wonderful days as well. None of us know what paths we'll cross in the next weeks or months. There will again be dark days and joyful days as well. All the intense pain we've felt just makes those future moments of joy that much stronger. In time, we'll all be together once again. Until then, we need to enjoy each moment we have. I ask God to give each of us the courage and strength that Nathaniel and John, and now Sam, have shown as they try to make a better life for us all."

The crackling of the fireplace was all that was heard for some time. As the night went on, Joseph fell asleep, and Mary carried him to his room. Shortly after, Rebeckah could fight her exhaustion no longer, and Sam carried her to her bed then retired himself. Lydia stayed with her mother for a while, neither speaking. Finally, she stood, kissed her mother on her forehead, and went to her room to sleep. Mrs. Mulliken sat alone, rocking slowly, deep in thought; her eyes welling with tears, she finally fell asleep in the chair.

The day for Sam to leave arrived. He had a few personal items in a canvas bag, and as Sam finished eating breakfast, Joseph came

CHAPTER 21

over to him and offered his fife. "You can take this with you so you can play it and think of me."

Sam smiled and gave it back. "No, little brother. Keep it and play it whenever you miss me. You will now be the man of the house. Mother and the girls will be depending on you."

"I'll take care of them, Sam." He turned and left the room.

Rebeckah also had a gift for him. She had a small fabric, white with the letters *S-A-M* stitched in black, with her initials in the corner. "I embroidered this for you," she said.

"Rebeckah, it's so special. I'll keep it with me everywhere I go." He hugged her.

After embracing his mother, Lydia, and Mary, Sam went outside to wait for the officer and other recruits. Rebeckah came out and stood by him. A few minutes later, a wagon approached, heading toward Cambridge. The officer was sitting in front, with six other men riding in back.

"Glad you decided to join us, young man. Climb aboard," the officer shouted.

Sam turned and looked at his mother, Lydia, Mary, and Joseph, who were standing at the front door. He tussled Rebeckah's hair and climbed onto the back of the wagon. As it rolled away, he waved at his family. The wagon rattled as it went down the road. Once it was out of sight, the family went inside, except Rebeckah. She stood at the wall for fifteen minutes, until Lydia came out to get her.

"Rebeckah, are you all right?" she asked, seeing her sister crying.

"Lydia, I love all my brothers, but Sam was my favorite," Rebeckah said through her tears.

"Oh, Rebeckah, I know," Lydia said, putting her arms around her sister. "It's okay to be sad. We can only keep him in our thoughts and prayers now until he comes home." The girls started inside. Lydia looked down the road, seeing the dust from the wagon in the distance.

As Lydia was heading to bed that night, she passed Rebeckah's room and heard her whispering in the dark. Lydia peeked around the door to Rebeckah's room and saw her kneeling next to her bed, praying. "Thank you, God, for my mother, sisters and brothers, and all that you have provided for us. But please, protect my brother Sam."

Chapter 22

September 1775

A large black crow soared above a group of majestic oaks, silhouetted against a bright-blue sky. He slowly and gracefully descended, landing on a large branch overlooking a peaceful cemetery and calling out to several comrades in a neighboring cornfield. A grey squirrel, fattened by the bountiful acorn crop of that season, scampered from tree to tree, while another hopped across the ground, looking for more nuts. In the distance, a long line of geese in the shape of a V could be heard honking as they headed south. The maples along the roadway had some early shades of deep crimson and fiery orange as they previewed the coming spectacle of autumn. A crisp, early fall day had come to Concord.

The sheer beauty and natural wonder of the late September day went unnoticed by Samuel Prescott. Gripped by the pain of sadness and loss, he mourned the passing of his closest brother and best friend, Abel Jr. What had appeared to be a minor wound that April morning several months earlier was apparently more significant, and Abel developed several internal infections, eventually leading to dysentery and a miserable death. Samuel had been notified by one of the Concord militia men that Abel had passed away, and the young doctor was given permission to leave the camp in Cambridge to spend time with his family.

Samuel sat alone—very alone—at their favorite table near the fireplace in Wright's Tavern, not even acknowledging the mug of warm ale slid onto the table in front of him by Amos Wright. Amos

CHAPTER 22

patted Samuel gently on the shoulder to console him. Abel had been Samuel's mentor, sharing his knowledge and experience just as their father and older brother, Benjamin, had done for Abel. They had shared so much over their lifetimes. They had been at this same table just months earlier with friends; now no one was here. Many of the younger men were with the militia outside Boston while others were busy trying to keep the town, their businesses or their farms functioning and helping others in the community survive. In Samuel's mind, he could hear Abel beckoning to friends or his hearty laugh as he told stories. Samuel sat there, missing the unspoken love and support of his older brother.

For the first time in months, his thoughts were not preoccupied with thoughts of Lydia. Not a moment had gone by since he left her at her house that he hadn't been consumed by worrying about her, missing her deeply, and wanting desperately to find her. This loss and the pain it caused was different but still overwhelming.

Reverend Emerson walked in, looking for Samuel. They had become close friends since the outbreak at the North Bridge, a friendship shaped through mutual respect and admiration. He had come looking for Samuel after stopping by the Prescott home to offer his condolences.

"My dear friend, how are you doing?" he asked softly as he sat next to Samuel.

"Reverend, I don't know how to grasp this. He didn't seem to be hurt that badly, and we all—three of us doctors—did what we knew to treat his injury and illness. My life will be so empty without him."

Reverend Emerson reminded him of the words of encouragement Samuel had given some of the wounded back in April, stressing that every morning brings a new day and each day is so precious.

"You have so much to offer the people of Concord, your family, and that young lady waiting for you. Take the time to reflect on Abel and treasure his memory, but he would want you to continue living your life with the same devotion and commitment that you both always had."

"Thank you, Reverend. It is just so hard."

The reverend put his arm around Samuel's shoulders, and they sat quietly for several minutes. Eventually, Samuel drank some of the ale, stood up, and told Reverend Emerson he was ready to go home. They waved at Amos Wright and left together, Samuel turning right to head home and Reverend Emerson going through the center toward his home near the bridge.

At the house, everyone was sad, but there was also concern for Mrs. Prescott. As Abel's condition had worsened, she had fallen into a deep depression. Her husband worried that losing Abel might have caused permanent emotional damage to her and could affect her physical health.

After Samuel returned from Wright's, he spent the rest of the day with his family, helping to care for his heartbroken mother. Before dark, Samuel headed back to camp. The emptiness in his gut from losing his brother haunted him, and he was consumed with worry about his mother as well. Samuel was at an emotional low point, feeling lonely without Lydia, sad about Abel, and feeling helpless with his mother's sadness. The sense of purpose he had always felt as a doctor was faltering; he thought of the failure to save his brother, his mother's emotional condition, and all the pain and suffering he had seen in his patients over the past six months. Those feelings stayed with him as he reached camp and went to sleep.

Chapter 23

November 1775
Late afternoon

As the beauty of fall and the colors of leaves faded away, they were replaced by the grey skies and cold of November. The people of the eastern part of the Massachusetts colony continued to struggle through the siege of Boston. Meanwhile, militia companies from several towns continued to surround the city, blockading the royal troops who never went further than the Charlestown peninsula after the horrific battle on Breed's Hill. Camps still created a twenty-mile circle around Boston.

Samuel continued treating the ill and injured in one of the camps, and late one afternoon, he requested permission from the commanding officer to visit another camp further north, where he believed many of the Lexington men were stationed.

"Be very careful, Doctor," the commander advised. "If you have anything to spare, take some extra supplies with you for whoever you are visiting. Try to get back before it gets too late."

Samuel saddled Duchess and headed north. As he rode into the camp, an armed guard at the entrance stopped him. "Halt," he demanded. "State your name and purpose of your visit."

"I am looking for the Lexington men. I am Dr. Samuel Prescott of Concord," he replied.

The guard lowered his musket, took off his hat, and let out a shout. "Dr. Prescott! It's me, David Quimby. You treated me at the North Bridge in April."

"David, what a surprise. How are you doing?"

"I am fine, thanks to you. A month after I was wounded, I was back on the road and joined the forces gathering here. I believe the men you're looking for are in the rear of the camp. If you have any trouble finding them, ask any of the men along the path."

"Thank you, David." Samuel tipped his hat.

David bowed, saying, "And thank you again, Doctor, for taking care of me."

"You're quite welcome, David. I wish you the best."

Samuel dismounted and led Duchess through camp. He wanted desperately to see Nathaniel and ask how he and his family were doing, especially Lydia. Three of the men Samuel passed suggested he look back in the sleeping area, saying the Lexington men were off duty and should be there.

As Samuel passed between rows of tents, he found Nathaniel sitting alone near a fire, his clothes slightly tattered and looking very thin and pale. Seeing a friendly face brightened his appearance instantly, though.

"By God, if it isn't Samuel Prescott!" Nathaniel said as he jumped to his feet. "It is so good to see you, my friend. How are you, and how have you been holding up through all of this?"

"I'm tired and hungry but very pleased to see you alive and well, Nathaniel. You look different from the last time I saw you."

"Buckman Tavern, midday in April. Ah, yes, I remember. Seems so long ago. Here, sit with me and tell me details of what's happened the past few months. Since the bitter battle on Breed's Hill back in June, I had been wondering how you were."

Samuel shook his head, saying, "I feared I would see you or John that day under dreadful circumstances. I'm glad both of you came through that battle unscathed." He looked down at Nathaniel's feet. "Is that a hole in your shoe?"

"Yes, haven't been able to get another pair. As long as my socks hold out, it will be all right. I just tie a rag around it when it rains." He laughed.

CHAPTER 23

Samuel went to his saddlebag and pulled out a couple more pairs of socks that he had packed. "I had heard many of you men were dealing with shortages, so brought these for you."

Nathaniel took them and thanked Samuel. They sat by the fire and shared stories of some of the events that had filled their days since June. Samuel gave him the terrible news about Abel, and Nathaniel told him he was worried about his two brothers, John and Sam, who had enlisted in the new Continental Army. They talked about their towns and the people they knew. However, Samuel's longing to discuss Lydia could not be held back any longer.

"Not to interrupt, Nathaniel, but have you had any word from your family—your sister in particular?"

"I was wondering when you would ask." Nathaniel laughed. "I spoke to some newly enlisted men last week who were being moved from Chelsea to New York. One of them had bought a clock from us last year, and he told me that my mother, sisters, and little brother had been moved from the house we found for them when they left Lexington to a former Tory's house somewhere farther from Lexington. Don't worry. Lydia is in a good, safe place for now, and she's probably thinking of you daily."

"My every thought is of her," Samuel said sadly. "How I wish this war could reach a desired end and we could all get back together in a more peaceful time."

"I understand how you feel. I worry about them all constantly. What are your plans going forward?"

"I was attending to one of General Washington's aides at his headquarters in the Vassal Mansion in Cambridge and overheard many of their concerns. Not enough weapons, shortage of clothing like shoes," Samuel said, pointing at Nathaniel's foot. "We need to have better defense, especially artillery, against the army still sitting in Boston. Colonel Knox is presenting a plan to General Washington to go to a fort in New York to get some additional cannons that could fortify our position and threaten the king's forces. I'm going to ask if they need a doctor to accompany them. Both Dr. Fiske and I have been appointed surgeons for the Continental Army, so I think I can help during the trip and maybe at the fort. I need a change of scenery and want to be more involved."

"Have you met General Washington yet?" Nathaniel asked. "I found him very impressive. He came to our camp to start new training practices."

"Yes, he seems to command the respect and loyalty of the officers and troops. Very similar to your Captain Parker."

Nathaniel lowered his head. "Guess you hadn't heard. Captain Parker passed away at the end of October. He had been dealing with consumption in his lungs since back in April but tried to keep it from all of us. And you're so right about lack of weapons and supplies. At one muster last week, some of the men were given spears as weapons as they had no ammunition."

Samuel shook his head. "Too bad about Captain Parker. He was a good man and a great leader. What are you doing about your enlistment? Doesn't it end at the end of the year?"

"Yes, but I want to see this through. We have all gone through too much for me to walk away now."

As darkness started to settle in, they sat quietly, reminiscing about a more peaceful time. While deep in conversation, Samuel looked up and saw a bright sky full of sparkling, shimmering stars.

"I wonder if she's looking at those stars tonight?' he said to himself, but it was just loud enough that Nathaniel could hear him.

"Since she was a little girl, she always loved to sit in the field and look at the stars," Nathaniel said. "I didn't know she had shared that with you."

They sat for some time in silence, deep in thought, listening to the crackling of the wood in the campfire.

"If you can somehow get word to her, please let her know I'm fine and that I miss her very much," Samuel said finally.

Nathaniel nodded. "I promise that I will."

As it was getting late, Samuel stood up. "I must be getting back. It was indeed a pleasure seeing you, Nathaniel. Stay well, and may God keep you safe."

"You too, my dear friend. Let's hope the next time that we meet, it can be to finalize the wedding. My sister deserves that. Once we

CHAPTER 23

can get this conflict resolved, we can all go back to our very ordinary lives."

They shook hands and then embraced. Samuel smiled weakly at Nathaniel before turning and walking between the tents and away from his friend.

Nathaniel watched as the doctor slowly mounted his horse, waved, and rode out of camp. He shivered as the chill in the air engulfed him. He was growing more tired each day and struggled to deal with the cold nights. His cough and the pain inside were becoming increasingly more difficult to bear, but it was refreshing to have part of his previous life pay a visit, even if for such a brief moment. He thought back to that warm house in Lexington that he had shared with his family and smiled as he fell asleep.

Chapter 24

Late November 1775–Spring 1776

The mission to Fort Ticonderoga was approved, and Samuel was asked to accompany the party led by Henry Knox. He welcomed the opportunity to get out of the camps and provide additional support to a cause for which he was becoming more passionate. As he went home to prepare for the long trip, there was one issue he had to resolve.

A rider and their favorite horse are inseparable. The trust and understanding built over time between a human and an animal can create a special bond. Samuel had developed that confidence and mutual respect with Duchess from so many trips—seeing patients, visiting Lydia, even casual rides. However, she was not the right horse for the tough expedition to Fort Ticonderoga. He needed a bigger, stronger, and more-durable horse for that long trip and tough conditions, so he decided on Rascal. A Percheron, larger and able to carry Samuel's supplies and clothing needed for the trip and indefinite stay, Rascal was gray, with a short black mane and black tail, and was younger than Duchess. He was also accustomed to a heavier workload but was also a good riding horse.

At home, while Samuel packed some clothing and supplies that he would need, his brother, Benjamin, brushed Rascal and prepared the horse for the trip. Samuel finished putting any important belongings, warmer clothing, and his medical supplies into a bag, planning to meet with Colonel Knox's company as they headed west out of Boston. As he said goodbye to his family, Samuel made a last-minute

CHAPTER 24

decision to use the half day he had left to make one more attempt to see Lydia. He desperately had to try to find her, to see her, just one time before he went on his way. He remembered that Elijah Sanderson knew where the family had gone that fateful day in April. Samuel rode into Lexington to find him and stopped at his cabinet shop.

"Dr. Prescott! Nice to see you again, sir," Elijah said as Samuel walked in.

"Nice to see you as well, Elijah. Hope you've been well. Could I trouble you for some assistance?" He asked Elijah for directions to the house where the Mullikens had gone, and Elijah made him a small map to the Latham farm. He also warned Samuel they were likely not there as they had moved into an abandoned house, but Myles would be able to take him to the new location.

"I have to at least try. Thank you, Elijah," Samuel said as he headed out.

"Good luck and God bless!" Elijah yelled as Samuel rode away.

Samuel followed the map for about an hour and saw a farm that resembled the one Elijah had described. Excited and a little eager, he jumped off Rascal even before the horse had completely stopped, running to the front door and pounding on it.

"Myles, Myles Latham! Can I speak to you please?" He knocked again after getting no response.

Unfortunately, no one was home. For only the second time in several years, Prudence had gone with Myles as he made his trip to Haverhill. Myles's friend, Joseph Burrill, had a tannery there and needed buckles for shoes the tannery was trying to sell to the Continental Army. In the past year, Myles had traded with him often to make the belts and leather aprons a blacksmith needed while Myles made the buckles. The Lathams had left early that morning and would be back the next day. There was no one there to let Samuel know how to find the Bagley property to which the Mullikens had relocated earlier.

Dejected and disappointed, Samuel walked around the side of the house just to be sure no one was there then climbed back onto Rascal and headed to his planned rendezvous with the Knox group heading west and eventually north. He caught up with them as they crossed into Framingham.

Colonel Knox acknowledged him. "Nice to see you, Dr. Prescott. Thank you for volunteering to join us."

"Thank you, sir. Please let me know how I can help."

The caravan headed west toward New York, being ferried across the Connecticut River just past Springfield. After handling the difficult passage through the Berkshires, they turned north, spending the night in Albany, where Colonel Knox failed at negotiating the purchase of animals to help pull the wagons that they would need to carry the cannons. Early the next morning, they continued going north and followed the Hudson River. Taking a brief stop outside Saratoga, Samuel quietly ate breakfast next to a campfire, listening to the yelping and howling of coyotes in the distance. There was still lingering disappointment that he didn't get to see Lydia before this mission, but he understood and welcomed the task at hand and tried to concentrate his energy on helping the soldiers during the tough winter trip and the eventual stay in Ticonderoga. His attention was brought back into focus by the squawking of a trio of blue jays on the edge of camp as one of the soldiers threw out a chunk of bread; Samuel watched as they fought over it.

The soldier nodded at Samuel. "Hope when this conflict finally ends, we colonists aren't the ones fighting for the last scraps of bread," the soldier said as he turned and returned to his unit.

As they approached Fort Ticonderoga later that afternoon, Samuel was in awe of what he saw. He had never seen a true fort, and this was truly impressive. Fieldstone walls mixed with plaster ranged from seven to forty feet high and ten to fourteen feet wide. It seemed impenetrable, and the cannon barrels protruding from the openings in the walls added to that impression. The points of the star-shaped fort had cannons facing in two directions, providing added protection by defending approaches from two sides.

Colonel Know and his team rode under the opening in the front wall into a large courtyard. A building, also constructed of fieldstones, was in front of them and ranging the length of the fort. It was used as barracks for the soldiers stationed there. Over to the right

CHAPTER 24

was a similar, but shorter, building where the officers stayed. It was in that area that Samuel was told to set up some space for himself. There was a military hospital in Fort George for serious illnesses, but his responsibilities at Ticonderoga were to handle the minor afflictions.

General Horatio Gates, the commanding officer, welcomed them. As soon as Colonel Knox had his group settled, Knox gave orders to his men to choose which of the cannons to take by alternating the arsenal in place so as not to weaken the fort's protection. This would get them about thirty cannons to go with another twenty or thirty that Knox knew were at Crown Point at the end of Lake Champlain. He had teams divided to allow the men to move the huge guns as easily as possible considering their immense weight. He also ordered some of his junior officers to go out to nearby farms and start gathering the wood and supplies to build the sleds and wagons which were needed to get the cannons back to Boston. They would also need to round up some oxen and horses from those farms to pull the sleds.

In the meantime, Dr. Prescott cleaned up a small room under the officers' barracks and set it up to see patients as needed. Supplies were limited to what he had brought or was able to find in the fort. Fortunately, most of his care over the next two weeks centered on splinters from building the sleds, broken feet from cannons being dropped on them, and an occasional bout of food poisoning.

Mealtime was surprisingly an improvement over the camps around Boston. The abundance of deer, turkeys, geese, and rabbits provided enough meat as well as the salmon and trout they caught from Lake Champlain. The now dormant garden outside the fort had supplied them with beets, potatoes, and carrots for the upcoming winter.

Only two weeks after arriving, Colonel Knox and his team were successful in preparing for the return trip. There was a sense of urgency to get the cannons back to Boston. They were fortunate to get a substantial snowstorm in time for the trip back, allowing easier movement of the sleds that carried the large and heavy cannons. Knox also took back with his company some barrels of powder and many muskets to help the cause.

Additional troops started flowing into the fort, many returning from the failed attempt to take Quebec. Samuel was asked by General Gates to stay to help the soldiers manage the winter and potential illnesses. He promised he would stay until summer and a replacement was on board. While the fort personnel dealt with the normal difficult, cold, and snowy weather expected in the Champlain area, spring eventually started to show signs of arriving. The snows eventually followed the expected routine of melting, plants began to sprout, and the days grew longer. Although Samuel started to feel that he had more of a purpose here at the fort, the emptiness was still lingering inside.

Chapter 25

February 1776

New England winters could be brutal. The heavy, wet snows put a stranglehold on everyday life. Howling winds felt as if they were blowing right through the body. The bitter cold, which seemed to last forever, could burn exposed flesh.

Occasionally, the harshness of winter was broken temporarily with a warm spell or with early springlike weather, with cold rain and dampness under heavy clouds. Such was the weather on the day when Nathaniel Mulliken was laid to rest.

During the siege of Boston, brother Sam had enlisted in the Continental Army and was deployed to help defend New York. John volunteered to go with him. Nathaniel thought it would be best if one of the three brothers stayed locally, helping to protect the area surrounding home in case the king's army ventured out of Boston again.

Nathaniel had celebrated with his fellow soldiers when Colonel Knox arrived with the cannons from Ticonderoga in mid-January. Although he was feeling weak, Nathaniel had volunteered to help get them deployed but found it was too much for him, and he had returned to camp. When the cannons were deployed overlooking Boston Harbor and the Royal Navy fleet, General Howe knew he could not defend against an attack. The general eventually ordered an evacuation of the city, sailing the military, their families, and any Loyalists to Halifax.

Nathaniel had tried to endure the "camp fever" that he was exposed to during the long siege, but it eventually took its toll. He passed away during the night, only six weeks before those cannons from Ticonderoga caused the British evacuation.

Nathaniel's body had been brought back to Lexington by a couple of the Lexington minutemen who knew his family and knew that they would want him to be buried properly. The men had approached Elijah Sanderson, knowing he could find the Mullikens and let them know what had happened. Once again, Elijah was assigned the unenviable task of delivering terrible news. He went to the Latham's to ask Myles to accompany him.

"Myles, you have become a great friend to the Mullikens. I need your help delivering some tragic news. Nathaniel has died."

"Oh no. That is terrible. I will do anything for that family. Can we do it right now?" Myles asked.

Elijah nodded, and they rode on his wagon to the house where the Mullikens were staying. Elijah did not like this troubling responsibility but handled it with care.

When Mary answered the door that morning, Elijah spoke carefully so they would understand the meaning of his words as well as his sorrow in having to deliver the message.

"My dear friends, I have been told by two of the minutemen who served with Nathaniel that he passed away quietly last week in camp. They have taken him to our meetinghouse, awaiting your ability to prepare him for his burial. I am so sorry to have to tell you such devastating news."

Mrs. Mulliken was heartbroken, but she told her family that Nathaniel was now with their father and at peace. They all cried while being consoled by Myles and Elijah.

Joseph asked his mother, "Is this one of those bad days you said might come?" Lydia comforted him.

Later that day, they went into Lexington to make final plans for Nathaniel.

Several of the townspeople, led by Reverend Jonas Clarke, joined the family on the dreary day of his burial. Nathaniel was buried in the Old Burying Ground just behind Jonathan Harrington's house,

CHAPTER 25

beside Nathaniel's father. Myles and Prudence Latham were there, as well as Elijah Sanderson, who stood with his arm around Mary.

Lydia trembled as she stood in the cold and misty morning air. The dark, wool coat she wore did little to fight the damp chill. She watched silently as the men lowered the wooden coffin into the black earth. It seemed like only yesterday that she had seen her father, Nathaniel, being buried on a morning like this. Now his oldest son, named for him, was being laid to rest next to him.

Their breath as they exhaled could be seen as the men began covering the casket, shovelful by shovelful. The earth overtook the cold, dark, silent hole. The sound of dirt and stones pelting the wooden box were soon replaced by the sound of muffled dirt on dirt. A stone with Nathaniel's name would be added in the coming days.

As the others, including her mother, sisters, and Joseph, turned and walked away, Lydia stood motionless and alone. She felt as if the moment was frozen in time. She heard nothing, sensed no one else around her. The heartache that gripped her like a vice was unlike anything she had ever felt. The loss of her dear older brother left her stunned and dazed. The pain inside was crushing.

When is all of this going to end? she thought silently. The rebellion and hardship had taken such a toll on all of them already in less than a year. Their house was gone; two of her brothers were somewhere out there fighting for what seemed like a hopeless cause. Nathaniel was now gone, and she hadn't seen her beloved Samuel for what seemed like an eternity. The massive weight of all this fell on her shoulders as she stood there alongside the fresh dirt, not knowing what to do or where to go. As the chill in the air finally brought her senses back, she turned and walked away. She understood and resigned herself to the fact that it was her responsibility to be strong for her mother and siblings, just as Nathaniel had been when they were all so much younger and their father had died.

Chapter 26

March 16–17, 1776

On a brisk Saturday morning in March, two figures emerged from the swirling snow that was blowing lightly along Hanover Street. They had walked up from the Common and were headed to Salem Street. Dressed in full regimental royal uniforms, they drew curious gazes from the people on the street and in shops along the road. One of the figures had a musket resting on his left shoulder; the other had a scabbard and sword hanging from his waist. Several of the people they passed smiled or nodded, but a few others looked at them with disgust. No one expected to see soldiers walking in this direction as everyone knew the evacuation of the city was beginning.

Since the cannons delivered by Henry Know from Ticonderoga had been placed on the hills overlooking Boston, the situation for the Royal Forces had become tenuous. General William Howe, now commander of the troops, had made plans to attempt an assault to remove them, but bad weather had canceled those plans. Cannon fire from the many warships in the harbor was ineffective as the hills were too high. Range was just right for the Continental battery if they fired from the heights, but trying to fire from ships uphill was useless. Hundreds of ineffective cannonballs were collected by colonial forces on the hillside.

With the addition of more cannons and fortifications on Dorchester Heights, it became apparent the city was no longer safe for the troops. Supplies, ammunition, and families of the soldiers

CHAPTER 26

had begun to be loaded onto ships as they made preparations to sail to Halifax. Many Loyalists were offered protection and passage as well.

The two soldiers walking along Hanover Street early that morning paid little attention to the residents as they passed. They turned into an alley that connected Hanover Street to Salem Street and continued until they reached the Old North Church. A man was sweeping snow off the steps leading to the front door of the church and saw them approaching.

The soldier with the sword removed his hat and spoke to the man. "Pardon me, good sir, but can you tell me where we can find church sexton Robert Newman?'

The man stared at the soldiers, looking them up and down for a minute. "And why would you need Mr. Newman?" he asked as he returned to sweeping.

The soldier who had spoken stepped forward. "I am Lieutenant William Pitcairn, and this is my brother, Thomas, sir. Our father, Major John Pitcairn, is in a tomb beneath this fine church. Before we leave Boston, we would like a moment to reflect at his tomb."

The man stopped and rested the broom against the side of the church. "I am Robert Newman, gentlemen. I knew your father well from his time attending our church. Disagreed with him and your king's treatment of our colony, but he was a good, fair, and decent man. I will be glad to take you down to his tomb." He paused, pointing at Thomas. "But that musket cannot come into the church. It must be left here."

"But I cannot leave it here in the street," Thomas protested, looking at his brother for support.

"Understood. I will find a safe spot for it just inside the door, out of view," Newman replied.

The three men entered the church through the front door with its arched transom window. Thomas handed his musket to Newman, who carefully placed it against a corner wall. He then gestured for the soldiers to follow him. They started down a series of wooden stairs toward the lower levels of the church. At the bottom of the stairs,

Newman removed a long metal key from a ring on his belt, unlocking a heavy wooden door.

When the door opened, the Pitcairn brothers were pushed back by the horrible stench of rotting skin and decaying bodies. The pungent odor was overwhelming as they entered the hallway.

"You get used to it after a while," Newman told them. "Follow me."

He lit the candle in a small black lantern that was hanging on the wall beside the door, taking it in his right hand and raising it above his head to lead the way. They started down the dark and narrow hallway, lined in brick including a low brick ceiling and held up with dark wooden timbers. The lantern flickered as they walked past tombs on either side of the hallway. The brothers looked up as they heard creaks and moans on the ceiling above them, but Newman just smiled.

"Probably the pastor walking between pews in the church. At least I hope that's what it is."

After making a few turns in the long hallway, Newman stopped at a tomb on the left, marked with a metal nameplate engraved with the words "Major John Pitcairn." The major had been interred with several of the other officers killed in the assault on Breed's Hill, but only his name was listed on the vault.

Newman used his lantern to light another on a hook on the wall, telling the brothers, "I will wait for you at the stairs. Bring this other lantern with you when you return." Then he turned and headed back.

"Wait! You're leaving us here?" a frightened Thomas asked.

"You are soldiers, for God's sake. No one here is going to harm you." Newman shook his head as he walked down the long dark hallway.

The brothers stood without speaking and with their heads bowed in the near dark of the hallway. After several moments, they stepped back, saluted their father's tomb, and made their way back up the hallway to the stairs, where Newman was waiting for them.

"Thank you, Mr. Newman," William said. "Your help was much appreciated."

CHAPTER 26

"I wouldn't have done it for anyone but you lads out of loyalty to your father. But I will be glad when all of you and your associates are out of Boston. I thought you would be gone by now."

"We were supposed to ship out yesterday, but the weather was uncooperative. I believe we are scheduled to sail tomorrow, winds permitting," William replied.

Newman nodded, turned, and led them upstairs. He handed the musket to Thomas, wished them well, and went into the nave of the church.

As they headed back toward the Common, Thomas looked at his brother and said, "Nice man, but a bit odd."

William nodded. "Lives with his mother in a boarding house that many of our officers used while stationed here. Father once told me he was suspected of helping alarm the countryside before the march to Concord last year by putting lanterns in the steeple as a message, but Newman put the blame on a captain of the militia, who had left town. At least he was kind enough to help us."

As they headed down Hanover Street, they were alarmed to see a mob of men blocking their path, many holding clubs and sticks.

Thomas lowered his musket, but William placed his hand on the barrel and said, "No, put it on your shoulder."

He then shouted to the men in front of them, "We don't want trouble."

One of the men stepped in front of the mob and shouted back, "You've all been nothing but trouble for the eight years you've occupied the city. This might be our last chance to get some vengeance for all the problems you have caused us."

As the mob moved forward, the brothers stepped back, trying to decide what to do next. As the mob came closer, the Pitcairns heard the crack of a pistol being fired behind them. They turned quickly to see another mob of men coming from the other direction. One man had pistols in each hand and was leading the way.

"Delvecchio and O'Leary, move aside and let these men through." He winked at the two brothers as he and the second mob passed, moving in front of the original mob. The man continued yelling at the other mob, "Let them pass or die here," he said, pointing the pistols at the leader of the first group.

Slowly the group of men moved to either side of the road, opening enough space for the two soldiers to walk through and continue their passage. They were yelled at, and many of the men spit on the ground as they passed. A snowball hit William on the back of the left shoulder, and a rock just missed Thomas's head as he tightened the grip on his musket. They avoided eye contact with the angry men around them while those who had come to their aid kept the mob at bay. When they were finally in a safe spot at a distance from the mob, they turned to thank the man and his group who had helped them.

"Thank you, my friend, for the very generous gesture," William said.

"Glad to help the king's men," the man said, bowing at his waist. "My name is Patrick Barnicle. Once you have squashed this foolish rebellion and return to London, tell the king I send my regards." He turned to walk away.

"Come with us, Mr. Barnicle," said Thomas. "We are helping many Loyalists find protection by leaving this city."

"Thank you, but no thanks. I am a lifelong Bostonian and will never leave, regardless of what the rebels in the colonies do. I will be here when you and your fellow troops return."

He waved to his men, and they headed back up Hanover Street. The brothers continued on their way, reaching the Common, where they nodded at each other and separated to join their units, with William returning to the Marines and Thomas to his army regiment. William and the Marines had been tasked to stay on shore until most of the 120 ships and 10,000 troops, with 1,000 Loyalists, had departed, as the last line of defense in the event any attacks were launched.

Sunday morning brought bright sunshine and favorable winds as the large fleet set sail. As one of the final warships pulled away from the docks and exited the harbor, Lieutenant William Pitcairn of the Royal Marines stood at the stern and looked up at the steeple of the Old North Church as it rose above the North End of Boston. He anticipated a return at some point in the expected battles to come

CHAPTER 26

but didn't know what the future held for his Marines or those now aboard ships. He lowered his head and shook it a few times, still grieving the loss of his father who had died on the hill across the river exactly nine months to the day.

At the same time, Henry Knox watched from the heights overlooking Boston Harbor, standing a few feet from several of the cannons he had moved from Ticonderoga. He knew that on board one of the ships below were his wife's parents and sister (who had married a Royal officer); he wondered if they would ever see each other again.

Outside the city, word of the completed evacuation was welcome news. The port would now be open to receive goods, and the markets in the city would again be available. Residents in many towns celebrated with relief the departure of the Royal Army and Navy, some firing muskets into the air. Myles brought the news to the Mullikens.

"Does that mean my brothers will be returning?" an excited Rebeckah asked.

"No, my dear. It is a little premature for celebrations. This conflict is far from over. It is just one small success, but there is still much to be done. There will be more dark days ahead."

PART 3

When in the Course of Human Events...

—Declaration of Independence

CHAPTER 27

Late Spring 1776–Summer 1776

At Ticonderoga, as the weather warmed and conditions improved outside the fort, General Gates ordered the building of additional fortifications on the eastern side of the lake across from the fort to protect the northern access. In July's heat, Samuel would spend his mornings walking along the top of the fort's walls. On one of these mornings, he noticed through the trees a solitary rider galloping up the hill outside the fort. The rider approached the fort, calling out for General Gates.

"I have an urgent message from General Washington regarding news from Philadelphia," he kept shouting. He was stopped at the entrance by one of the guards until General Gates could be summoned. Samuel leaned over the wall in one of the cannon openings so he could hear the conversation below.

General Gates, accompanied by several of his officers, came to meet the courier. "I am General Gates, my friend. What news do you have for me?"

The young man saluted and handed him a packet that included a scrolled document. The general glanced through the papers and unrolled the scroll. He smiled, rolled the document up, and yelled out to one of the sentries, "Howard, get this fine young man some water, as well as some for his horse."

General Gates ordered the officers to gather the troops and staff, including Samuel, and requested one of the officers to read to them the document delivered by the courier—the Declaration

CHAPTER 27

of Independence that had been signed in Philadelphia earlier that month. The work being done on the fortifications across from Ticonderoga would eventually be named Mount Independence.

Once the men were assembled so they could all hear him, General Gates held up a copy of the document. "What we are about to read to you is a declaration to the world that we are no longer going to be abused by the king and that, as free people, we are asserting our rights. I wanted each of you to hear the commitment and determination as stated by the men at the Second Continental Congress."

He gave the document to General Arthur St. Clair who climbed up on a large boulder at the edge of the construction area, stood before them, and began reading. His words were firm and loud so all could hear. "*In Congress, July 4, 1776. The unanimous Declaration of the thirteen united States of America.*"

St. Clair paused and took a deep breath, then started reading again:

> *When in the course of human events, it becomes necessary for one people to dissolve the political bands which have connected them with another, and to assume among the Powers of the earth, the separate and equal station to which the Laws of Nature and of Nature's God entitle them, a decent respect to the opinions of mankind requires that they should declare the causes which impel them to the separation.*

The general paused for a moment, looking into the faces of the men before him. He wanted to be sure they were understanding all that he was reading. Then he continued:

> *We hold these truths to be self-evident, that all men are created equal, that they are endowed by their Creator with certain unalienable Rights, that among these are Life, Liberty, and the pursuit of Happiness. That to secure these rights, Governments*

are instituted among Men, deriving their just powers from the consent of the governed. That whenever any Form of Government becomes destructive of these ends, it is the Right of the People to alter or to abolish it, and to institute new Government, laying the foundation on such principles and organizing its powers in such form, as to them shall seem most likely to effect their Safety and Happiness.

Several of the men near Samuel grunted agreement as General St. Clair started to carefully read the long section that detailed the grievances of the colonies. It was amazing to see the passion and enthusiasm building as the general proceeded through the resolution. His voice filled with emotion, the general finally reached the last section of the document. He deliberately articulated each word, trying to express the deep meaning of every sentence as he finished reading:

We, therefore, the Representatives of the united States of America, in General Congress, Assembled, appealing to the Supreme Judge of the world for the rectitude of our intentions, do, in the Name, and by authority of the good People of these Colonies, solemnly publish and declare, That these United Colonies are, and of Right ought to be Free and Independent States; that they are Absolved from all Allegiances to the British Crown, and that all political connection between them and the State of Great Britain, is and ought to be totally dissolved; and that as Free and Independent States, they have full power to levy War, conclude Peace, contract Alliances, establish Commerce, and to do all other Acts and Things which Independent States may of right do. And for the support of this Declaration, with a firm reliance on the Protection of Divine

CHAPTER 27

Providence, we mutually pledge to each other our Lives, our Fortunes, and our sacred Honor.

When St. Clair had finished, he remained quiet and serious, holding the document high above his head for all to see.

As the reading concluded, Samuel could see tears in the eyes of some of the men while many others were nodding vigorously in agreement with what they had just heard. Spontaneously, a loud cheer came up from the gathered soldiers. General Gates and his officers walked through the gathering of these ordinary men, united together in something they all were fighting for, shaking hands and giving words of gratitude and encouragement.

Samuel met Gates as he prepared to return to the fort. He smiled at the general, telling him, "They needed that, sir."

General Gates looked at him and said, "Doctor Prescott, these men—all of us—have been away from homes and families for a year or more. I hope this will remind them why we are here together, working toward a common cause, our glorious cause."

One night later that week, Samuel was walking through the courtyard returning from a late dinner. He always found nighttime a little disconcerting when there was a full moon over the fort (as there was that night) as it created shadows that moved along the walls and edges of the buildings; it seemed like the spirits of former warriors of the fort were watching over the current occupants. As Samuel passed the officers' quarters, he jumped back as General Gates came out of a shadow in front of him.

"Dr. Prescott, good evening." The commander hadn't noticed that Samuel had jumped back.

"Good evening, sir."

"I know your plans are to leave soon. We have a contingent of soldiers and other people from Massachusetts joining us in about a week. Can you stay until then? I believe there may be a doctor among the group. You can transfer your services to him at that point."

"Of course, sir. I have no immediate need to depart. Let me know when they arrive, and I will be glad to welcome them."

Gates continued, "And by the way, in case you haven't heard, the mission that brought you here was apparently very successful. When Colonel Knox returned with the cannons and they were deployed on the heights overlooking Boston, the British were forced to evacuate. Earned him a promotion to general."

"That's wonderful news. Thank you for letting me know." As the general walked away, Samuel retired to his quarters.

As General Gates had said, a week later, one of the sentries signaled that a group of men was approaching. The guards were alerted in case they were foe, but it was the next group of soldiers being stationed at the fort. Samuel was standing outside his infirmary, waiting for orders, when he was stunned by the sound of a familiar voice.

"Dr. Samuel Prescott! I thought you might be here. Actually, I was truly hoping you would be. So glad to see you!"

Samuel was shocked; it was Reverend William Emerson.

"Dear God, what are you doing here, Reverend?" Samuel embraced him.

"I'm a chaplain for the Continental Army, and they asked me to accompany this group of men and help them get settled. It will be nice to spend time with you."

"I was supposed to leave after your arrival. Do you have a doctor in your party?"

"We did, but the fool fell off his horse leaving Albany, and we left him there to recover. Should be here later this summer. Can you stay?"

"Of course, I will, since you are here now. It will be nice to have a friendly face around."

Samuel showed Reverend Emerson around, introduced him to some of the officers and men, and they enjoyed some time talking before retiring for the night.

They shared their evening meals each night. After one dinner, Samuel sat with Reverend Emerson, very quiet and deep in thought; his friend Emerson noticed.

"Thinking of your Miss Mulliken?" Emerson asked.

"I do that constantly," Samuel said, smiling. "But no, I've been having some concerns and second thoughts about my role in

CHAPTER 27

this rebellion. Since I was young, I had always wanted to follow in my father's footsteps and be a doctor, Then, as I grew older, I was inspired by my two older brothers and their love of their profession. I'm happy and fulfilled helping the many soldiers here, and their appreciation and support has been wonderful. But I'm getting weary of treating the same issues every day. I feel I should be, and could be, doing more for the cause. I remember the commitment of Dr. Warren, and I feel as though I'm not doing enough."

"My Lord, Samuel, you have done so much! I saw how you helped that day in Concord last April. You were tireless in the camps around Boston during the siege. And during the Breed's Hill battle, you did all you could for those wounded men. I have always been amazed at your commitment."

"I appreciate you saying that, but treating one patient at a time has had such little impact compared to the efforts of the men I have helped."

"Are you considering joining the army?" Reverend Emerson asked, surprised.

"No, but I feel as though I can do more. I keep thinking I'm going through life completing tasks, accepting my responsibility, and missing out on a deeper inner purpose. I have seen that in the men I have helped. They are driven with such commitment and passion. They need help in other ways. I remember, when I was in Cambridge, I overheard General Washington and his officers bemoaning the fact that the Continental Army is in desperate need of weapons, the soldiers have such tattered and insufficient clothing, and other supplies are so short. I had actually taken some of my father's supplies from home to help supplement the needs of the doctors during the siege. I know the Continental Congress has worked diligently to keep up with the army's demands, but everyone is struggling."

A soldier at the end of the table who had been listening to their conversation put down his cup to speak. "Doctor, the Congress has only so many resources. But there is a way you can help if you're serious."

Samuel looked over at Reverend Emerson and turned then to the soldier. "Can you explain?"

The soldier stood up and walked over to them, sitting across from Samuel, next to Reverend Emerson. "I am with the New Hampshire forces who came here recently. My name is Matthew Willis. My brother has been overseeing a project commissioned by the Congress to intercept supplies shipped to the Royal Forces from England. His ships have been increasingly successful providing additional aid to our army."

"Are you talking about the Continental Navy?" asked Reverend Emerson.

"No, hardly. The Continental Navy has had more trouble than the army getting and keeping men. This is a private business."

"Sounds like pirates to me," Samuel said, a bit insulted.

"No, Doctor, pirates steal from ships and have no loyalty to anyone but themselves. These men are patriots who prevent weapons and supplies from reaching the enemy, transfer them to our side, and get compensated for their work. It's all authorized and recognized by the governing bodies of the colonies. They are privateers, not pirates."

Samuel still wasn't convinced. "I don't see how that can have much impact, Matthew."

Matthew smiled and continued. "Well, just to give you an idea, in the past year, several of these privateers have had much success. One captured ship provided two thousand muskets, thirty-one tons of musket balls, one hundred thousand flints, and a hundred barrels of powder. General Washington actually cheered when he received the manifest listing the goods."

Samuel and Reverend Emerson were impressed. "Come to think of it, I remember my brother Benjamin mentioning that some of their medical stock had come from Portsmouth after a ship carrying supplies for the army was intercepted off the coast of Maine. I guess I'll need to think about it some more. How would I go about getting involved?" Samuel asked.

"My brother works out of both Macchias and Portsmouth, but it's best to find him in Portsmouth when you decide. Here. I will write down details for future reference if you need it." He went to an officer for some paper and scribbled a note for Samuel.

CHAPTER 27

"His name is Morgan Willis, and he can usually be found by speaking to John Moffatt on Fore Street in Portsmouth. John is an elderly wealthy man, former seaman, who can put you in touch with Morgan. When you get to Portsmouth, ask for location of John's house—very prominent in town, and everyone will know where it is—and speak to his house manager, Prince Whipple."

"Thank you, Matthew. But if this is your brother's business and is so worthwhile, why are you here?"

Matthew laughed. "I was born and raised in the White Mountains. I have no desire to be stuck on a ship surrounded by water, and I definitely don't need my younger brother as my boss." He said goodbye to the two friends and left. Reverend Emerson asked Samuel what he was going to do.

Samuel shrugged. "I have to think about it. A wise man I know once gave a sermon that we are put on this earth for a reason. Some of us may spend our whole life searching for that purpose. Maybe that's what I'm doing—longing to find that purpose for why I am here."

Reverend Emerson smiled. "I can't believe you remembered that part of my first sermon when I came to Concord. Glad you heard me and it affected someone in my congregation."

"You've said many things in your time in Concord that affected me and others," Samuel said as he stood up to leave. "I'm committed to be here for the summer anyways. That will give me some time to decide. It's not as though this war is ending anytime soon anyways."

"The Lord will guide you in the right direction. Think it through and decide what path your life needs to follow to find that inner purpose you long for," said Reverend Emerson as he rose. They left and walked through the fort.

Arriving at the sleeping quarters, they parted for the night. Samuel thought about the discussion throughout a long night.

Chapter 28

August 1776

War has a way of creating turmoil and disruption in even the simplest of life's activities. Throughout the colonies, fields were left unplowed while the farmers were in some distant location, fighting for a common cause. Shops that had been bustling in towns and villages before the march on Concord were mostly closed. Church services had fewer parishioners, mostly older people, women, and children. But no matter the conflict, some things never change; families need to take care of each other. The seasons continue to evolve, with winter's snows melting into lush springs, and eventually hot and humid summers.

On such a summer day, the bright sun baked the dry, dusty earth as a tired and sweaty Lydia worked in a small garden behind the house. Mary had taken the two youngest into town to try and barter some of their crops for sugar and flour. Lydia shooed a couple of small rabbits out of the garden and dodged a plump bumblebee as it hurriedly made its way from the coneflowers to its hive. She picked a handful of beans and discarded some broken plants into a compost pile on the outer edge of the garden. Stopping briefly to wipe her brow, Lydia was stunned to see several men on horses riding into the yard in uniforms belonging to the king's army.

"Good afternoon, madam," a young officer said as he dismounted. "We're part of a detachment marching from Canada to reinforce our forces in New York. On orders from the king, we are here to gather some supplies for our camp."

CHAPTER 28

"Well, sir, we have barely enough for ourselves. You'll have to tell King George to send you some supplies from his palace in England." She turned and walked away.

"Ah, another rebel, are you? We shall see what supplies you have." Turning to his men, he shouted, "Search the house and the barn. Do not destroy any personal property, but take whatever food, water, or weapons you find."

Lydia stared at him with hate in her eyes. "Why don't you just leave us alone?"

He ignored her and walked toward the house while several of his men spread out on their search. Lydia suddenly thought of the extra musket balls and axes Sam and Myles had hidden for any militia that might pass and need them. Trying to be as inconspicuous as possible, she strolled toward the rear of the barn where the items were stored in a wooden box under a manure pile. Glancing to make sure none of the soldiers could see where she had gone, she was startled to see the corner of the storage box had been exposed by recent rains. Lydia quietly began pushing some dirt and manure with her foot toward the exposed corner of the box. It was just a little too high to be done in this way, so she stooped and took a handful of dirt to cover the exposed area.

Satisfied that it was no longer visible, Lydia turned to go back in front. As she turned, she found a pistol was pointing at her eyes.

"Well, what have we here? Are you hiding something, my little rebel?" It was the officer.

"I don't know what you mean, sir," Lydia said cautiously. She had never had a weapon that close to her face.

Suddenly, from around the corner of the barn, Mrs. Mulliken ran toward the officer, armed with a long pitchfork. "Leave her alone!" she shouted.

One of the soldiers standing guard near the horses saw Mrs. Mulliken and raised his musket, aiming it at the older woman as she approached the officer. Just as he squeezed the trigger on his gun, a sword crashed down on it, causing him to fire into the ground. The sound of the shot stopped everyone.

A senior British officer who had come across the scene shouted at the young officer. "Put that pistol away!"

"Yes, Captain. But I believe we may have people here who are aiding the enemy." He looked at Lydia with a stare full of contempt and disgust.

"Nonetheless, Lieutenant, your job here was to round up supplies. I'm sure these ladies were not such a danger to you and your troops that your guns were needed. Get your men together," he ordered, the anger showing in his voice.

The older officer dismounted his horse and approached Lydia and her mother. "Madam, I apologize for the behavior of these men. I assure you that the king's army means you no harm."

"The king's army has already harmed us, sir. Some of your troops burned down our house. My oldest son is cold in the ground, and two others are out there somewhere, fighting your troops." Mrs. Mulliken looked up at him proudly as she spoke of her sons. "It would have been an honor to shove this pitchfork through that pitiful young officer."

The man was caught a little off guard. "I'm truly sorry to hear of your loss, but though enemies, we share in the grief of war. My only son, my purpose for being here in the colonies, was killed at the battle on Breed's Hill a year ago. This has been difficult for all of us."

He removed his hat and bowed. "Please excuse us for bothering you." Turning, he ordered, "Lieutenant, take whatever food supplies you found, but leave any meat or water here."

The captain mounted his horse, gave marching orders to the men, and they all rode away. Lydia stared at them, shaking her head in disgust, as they disappeared into the horizon. How she wished her brothers had been there to confront them.

Day after day passed, and they all missed having the older brothers around the house to help with the daily chores. Despite much help from Myles, Mrs. Mulliken, Mary, and Lydia worked very hard each day keeping their household and gardens safe and functioning; even young Rebeckah and Joseph contributed where they could. It was grueling work, and they all went to bed each night extremely tired.

CHAPTER 28

One night, after Lydia made sure the house was in order and everyone had retired for the evening, she climbed into bed exhausted, thinking about the visit of the soldiers a week earlier. How she wished John and Sam would come home soon. And as she did every night, Lydia thought about Samuel. Resting her head on her pillow, on the verge of sleep, her mind flashed back to a quieter and happier time. It was a day that she had fond memories of frequently, a day in late December 1774, before all of this had changed their lives.

It was a Sunday afternoon, and Samuel had accompanied her to services at the meetinghouse on the Green. He was walking her home, and as they left the Green, a soft, gentle snow began to fall. She cuddled closer to Samuel to stay warm, her right hand tightly gripping his left arm. He looked down at her and reached over with his right hand to place it on hers.

"Lydia, your hand is so cold!" he said. "Are you all right?"

"I'm fine, Samuel. It's just getting cold, but as long as you are here with me, I'll be warm enough."

"Here, give me your hands." He cupped his hands around hers and softly blew on them to try to warm them. As he did, she gently kissed him on his neck just below his left ear. He kissed her on her forehead.

Samuel smiled down at her, watching as the snowflakes floated down, landing delicately on her eyebrows and eyelashes then melting away. He gazed into her eyes and quietly asked, "Lydia, would you do me the honor of becoming my wife?"

Lydia looked up at him, the sparkle in her eyes showing wonder and joy at what he had just asked her. "I've hoped you would ask me that since the day you helped my little brother, Joseph, get home. There is nothing that would bring me as much joy and happiness as spending the rest of my life with you. Of course, I will!"

She threw her arms around his neck and held him tightly as they both ignored the snow falling faster around them.

The exhaustion of the day's work finally overcame her. In the darkness and comforted by her memories, Lydia fell asleep. The stillness of the night was broken occasionally by the serenading of several crickets outside her window.

Chapter 29

Late summer 1776

The uncertainty of life produces many twists and turns, bringing great joy or profound sadness. Often and unfortunately, the time spent with friends and loved ones can be fleeting. One hot summer day, Samuel had an unexpected patient show up at the infirmary—his friend, Reverend Emerson. The reverend had started to have bouts of diarrhea with stomach cramps and was getting weaker. Samuel examined his friend, inquired about what he had been eating, and expressed concern that the reverend could have early signs of dysentery. They decided together that it would be watched carefully over the next couple of weeks, with Samuel continuing to examine him as needed.

In the weeks to follow, Reverend Emerson's illness worsened. He eventually stopped joining Samuel for meals and even missed Sunday service. One night, a soldier stopped to see Dr. Prescott and said the reverend had asked if Samuel could come see him.

As he entered his friend's room, Samuel could sense it was getting serious. Reverend Emerson brightened slightly once he saw Samuel.

"I'm so glad you came. I need to ask a favor."

"Anything for you—you know that," said Samuel, sitting by him.

"I don't want to die here. I am planning on leaving the fort in the next day or two and will try to get home to spend some time with Phebe before I die. Have you decided on what path you want to

CHAPTER 29

take? Are you still considering meeting Morgan Willis in Portsmouth at some point?"

"Yes, but not until my replacement arrives from Albany. Why?"

"Will you help me get back to Concord?"

"Are you sure you can travel? You're getting very weak."

"I want to try. I received permission from General Gates. He said he would grant you his approval as well if you wanted to accompany me. The other doctor we left behind in Albany is on his way here and should arrive in the next day or two. Because of growing hostilities in the New York area, the general said he would send two armed soldiers with us for protection. They are Massachusetts men from Lunenburg who are needed by their commander, so they were heading back anyway."

"Let me get my things together. We can leave tomorrow." Samuel placed his hand on his friend's forearm. "I'm sorry you're dealing with this, my dear friend."

"We all have crosses to bear, Samuel. Let me rest and tell me when you are ready tomorrow."

In the morning, accompanied by Greydon Pike and Seth Taylor, the two guards assigned to them for protection, Samuel and Reverend Emerson left the fort. The group followed Otter Creek south and then headed east into the New Hampshire Grants to avoid the building British forces along the Hudson River. Dr. Prescott continually checked with Reverend Emerson to make sure the trip was not too much, but they could only get as far as Rutland as the reverend's condition worsened. Reverend Emerson knew the local pastor, Benajah Roots, in Rutland, and they all stayed a few nights at his house.

During the stay, Reverend Emerson continued to fail. His dysentery was destroying his body, and the cramping made him weaken considerably. He called for Samuel one morning.

"My friend, I don't believe I have much longer, and will not be able to go on. Please continue on your trip to Portsmouth. These fine gentlemen will take my belongings back to Concord and let Phebe know what happened." He pointed at Greydon and Seth, waiting outside his door. They both nodded in agreement.

"Seriously? I cannot leave you," Samuel insisted. "You have been with me through some tough times, tragic moments in my life, and I won't leave you here now."

"My dear, dear friend, remember to finish your search, not only for your true purpose but for your dear Lydia. Let me die in peace, knowing you continued on your quest."

Samuel was torn. He knew there was nothing else he could do for his friend, but he did not want to leave him. Reverend Emerson kept insisting, and Samuel finally agreed.

"I won't argue with you, my friend. Please rest and find peace, William." It was the first time he had called him by his first name in their relationship. "Thank you for your friendship and your guidance."

"May the Lord be with you, Samuel. And thank you for everything you have done. You're a fine man and a true friend. Have a safe and successful journey as you start a new chapter in your life."

Samuel went outside the room and spoke with Greydon and Seth, who promised they would continue the trip to Concord with Reverend Emerson's belongings and let his family know what had happened. He also said goodbye and thanked Pastor Roots, who assured him that Reverend Emerson would be buried properly in a family site on the property. The pastor suggested he go southeast to the small town of Springfield on the border with New Hampshire, where he could get a ferry across the Connecticut River to Charlestown, New Hampshire, then head east to continue on his way. Samuel mounted Rascal, left Rutland, and started on his way. He found the Wentworth ferry suggested by Pastor Roots and was fortunate that the river was lower than usual due to a dry summer, making the trip across uneventful. The raftlike ferry was poled across to the New Hampshire side, and he continued on his way. Samuel rode throughout the day, thinking about his friend, William Emerson, and his worsening condition. There was a soft mist as the dreary day wore on, making the day even gloomier for him as he rode alone. He stopped briefly while several turkeys crossed the road in front of him. While the hens seemed oblivious to the fact that he was there, a large tom turkey blocked his path. It puffed up its chest

CHAPTER 29

feathers and spread wide its tail feathers in an attempt to look larger and menacing. It made Samuel smile, finally lightening his mood after some troubling days.

"Move on, my friend. I intend no harm to you or your brood." Samuel waved his arm, and eventually, the turkey meandered into the woods following the hens.

Samuel kept going until the gathering darkness made it difficult for him to see the roadway, and he stopped outside Derryfield (now Manchester), New Hampshire, at an inn just west of the Merrimack River.

It was a restless, sleepless night for him. He had just left a great friend on his deathbed, still carried the pain of losing his dear brother, Abel Jr., and the ongoing anguish over not being able to see, to hold, his Lydia continued to overwhelm his thoughts. Maybe, he thought, he should give up this idea of going to sea and instead head south, return to Concord and his medical profession, find Lydia, and move forward with their life together. Was that a better choice, or should he continue to Portsmouth, fulfilling a deep desire to honor his brother's commitment to the cause, one also shared passionately by Reverend Emerson and Lydia's brothers? If he continued to the coast, perhaps he could see how he felt after meeting with Morgan Willis—or was it a waste of precious time? Could it provide a better life for him and Lydia, especially in a world potentially free from British tyranny and a more-hopeful future? Samuel was tormented with these thoughts, feeling alone and lost. During the tortuous night, he recalled a sermon Reverend Emerson had given on the Sunday just before the events on that fateful April day:

"There is often an internal struggle with choices one has to make. Is this decision what is best for me as an individual, or will it be better for the greater good of the community? True leaders often decide based upon the impact on the community, disregarding their own self-interests. Some false leaders have no conflict at all—they simply pursue what most benefits them, regardless of its possible detrimental effect on others. Our present king exemplifies this selfish approach. The best among us try to find a balance with mutual benefits for themselves as well for those

around them. We must all weigh this balance carefully as we decide on the paths presented to us daily."

As dawn came and he laid there, struggling with the decision, Samuel got up, dressed, and set out with Rascal, not sure what direction to take. He rode south to Reed's Ferry Landing, reaching the edge of the Merrimack River, trying to decide whether to cross and continue toward Portsmouth or stay on this side of the river and ride south toward Massachusetts. Still struggling with the choice, Samuel remembered Reverend Emerson telling him he had to find his purpose in life, as well as the sacrifices that his brother and so many of the militia had made in his presence for a cause they believed in. His heart pulled at him to just head south and return to Concord and Lydia. But he also felt a burning passion that had been growing over time, with every soldier he had treated, his memory of Abel, and the commitment he had seen from Reverend Emerson. This internal desire told him it was necessary to move forward to find an answer to his destiny. If he was to calm the inner confusion and indecision, he needed to go on. Samuel decided to cross the river and continue eastward. He convinced himself that the final decision could wait until he had more information after he spoke with Morgan Willis.

The ferry this time was more adventurous. It was a long, flat-bottom boat, about twenty feet long, eight feet across. Samuel stood next to Rascal, holding the reins, as they were joined by a farmer with four sheep also crossing at that time. Two men with poles, one on each end, struggled to keep the boat heading forward, fighting a strong current. Rascal snorted a couple of times, feeling unsteady, but Samuel stroked his snout to keep him calm. Eventually, the ferry reached the shore on the Litchfield side of the river, and Samuel led Rascal ashore, relieved the crossing was over. He let his horse drink from the river momentarily then headed east.

Samuel made it to Portsmouth later that day. He inquired where he could find John Moffatt and was directed to a fine home on Fore Street. It was a three-story Georgian, one of the tallest homes Samuel had ever seen. There was an ornate portico over the front door, supported by two columns. Samuel knocked at the door and was greeted by a well-dressed black man.

CHAPTER 29

"Are you Prince Whipple?" Samuel asked.

"No, sir, Prince has gone with Mr. Whipple to discuss business affairs in Derryfield. I am Windsor Moffatt, his assistant."

Samuel explained he was looking for John Moffatt.

"Come in, sir. Mr. Moffatt is outside in the garden."

As they walked through the striking entry hall, Samuel was amazed at the grand staircase with a curved banister leading upstairs. Windsor led him outside to find Mr. Moffatt, who was sitting in an old chair in the garden. Mr. Moffatt welcomed him and asked him how he could be of assistance.

"Mr. Moffatt, my name is Samuel Prescott. I was told by Matthew Willis that you might be able to help me meet with his brother Morgan?"

"Yes, Mr. Prescott. Please, sit with me."

"I am very impressed with your house, sir. And you must enjoy these gardens," Samuel said as he looked around the property.

"I built the house as a gift for my son. His name was also Samuel, but I won't hold that against you," he said, smiling. "He squandered his fortune and moved away, so I came here to live with my daughter after she married William. I can use the widow's walk on top to look down on the wharves. I spent many years down there."

John was getting older and struggled with his hearing, so he thought being outside would not disturb his daughter, Katharine. He raised his voice to speak to Samuel. "Do you know what Morgan does?" asked Mr. Moffatt, wanting to be sure of Samuel's intentions.

"Yes, sir," Samuel replied. "I understand he runs a business that includes ships to intercept royal supplies and channel them to the Continental forces. Is that a problem?"

John leaned toward Samuel so he could better hear him, saying, "No, no, Samuel. I support the work he does. My son-in-law, William Whipple, is a representative from New Hampshire to the Continental Congress and was one of the signers of our wonderful Declaration back in July. He returned from that event several weeks later and actually planted seeds of a horse chestnut tree from Philadelphia just behind you to remember the event. Not much growing yet, but he hopes it will be a great tribute to his participation. I hope I live long enough to see it at least come out of the ground. And see that damask rose bush behind you? Damn thing attracts too many bees all summer. Planted by my ex-daughter-in-law. It came from England. I should probably burn the damn thing down."

They both laughed, and the older man continued, "I'm pleased to help you get involved. Both my son-in-law and I have spent years as seafarers, some of the best years of my life. I envy you and know you will find the experience enriching."

"Thank you, sir. Do you want to go back inside?"

"No, I like to sit here in the ocean air and watch the waves come and go. Day after day slowly passes with nothing new, no surprises, no joy, no sorrow. I'm just biding my time until my time here comes to an end." His voice slowly trailed off, and he looked off into the distance.

After taking a deep breath and sighing, he told Samuel, "I'll tell Windsor to find Morgan and have him meet you, probably about dusk, at the Earl of Halifax Tavern on Queen Street, along the shore. Wait outside of the tavern. Many loyalists spend time there, and you don't want to have to explain why you are there. You'll recognize Morgan by his long gray beard and red complexion."

Later that evening, Samuel waited at the tavern, just along the edge of the Piscataway River as it flowed into the Atlantic Ocean. A man walked up to him as darkness started to show on the horizon and introduced himself.

"Dr. Prescott, I assume? I'm Morgan Willis." He extended his right hand.

Samuel shook his hand. Morgan looked exactly like John Moffat had described him. The man had a very strong grip and put his left hand over Samuel's hand. They went inside, walking to a back corner.

"Please, sit. I understand you met my older brother, Matthew. How can I help?"

"I was intrigued by the stories your brother told me about your efforts and how you interfere with British deliveries of goods," Samuel replied. "I'm looking for a way to be more involved in the cause."

CHAPTER 29

Morgan looked at him closely, examining his eyes, before sitting back in his chair. "Are you serious about this? I know you're a doctor, and this will be much different than the life you have lived."

"I'm tired of dealing with disease, performing amputations, and other medical work without proper equipment and supplies. I'm also tired of seeing hardworking, determined men armed with old, damaged weapons and a lack of clothing and food. I want to help." Samuel's sincerity impressed Morgan. "Is this a lifetime commitment?" Samuel asked.

Morgan shook his head. "No, I want people who enjoy this work, not someone to cause trouble. If you decide after a couple of voyages that it isn't for you, just let me know." He leaned in slightly, glancing over his shoulder then looking back at Samuel.

"John Stavers, the owner here, is suspected of favoring Loyalists, so we should be careful how much we say."

"Understood," Samuel replied. "But I'm serious about helping the cause."

"Great. We can use someone like you. I own two ships of crews doing this work. One sails out of Marblehead, the *Freedom*, captained by Maxwell Dodd. The other is a ship leaving in two days from here in town. It sails the coastline from Gloucester and north as far as Calais, depending on prevailing winds and the tides. Ship superstitions dictate that it departs on a Sunday. It was already fully manned, but having a ship doctor wouldn't hurt. You can still use your knowledge and skills, even on a limited basis. Come back here in the morning, and I'll introduce you to the captain."

They stood up, shook hands again, and left. Samuel returned to his lodging, determined to make this opportunity work.

When he rose in the morning, a cold October day dawned along the coastline. Samuel made his way back to the tavern. Morgan and another man were waiting on the cobblestone street outside and greeted him.

"Mr. Prescott, this is Captain Peter Lucas Grant, commander of the *Gryphon*, the ship I was telling you about last night."

Samuel shook the man's hand. "Nice to meet you, Captain Grant. Why did you name your ship the *Gryphon*?"

The older man laughed and explained. "In mythology, the gryphon was the guardian of treasures and priceless possessions. It also symbolized strength and courage. We believe the goods we intercept are treasures and priceless to the Continental forces, and it takes strength and courage to do what we do!"

They went inside to share breakfast and talk. Samuel asked about the crew of the ship. Captain Grant reviewed his staff for Samuel. "My first mate is a young man from Salem named Patrick Davis. He had done some work with the Pickerings but has been with me for a while. We have a man from the Mediterranean called Bela. He's the ship's carpenter and maybe the strongest man you'll ever meet. Michael Ross is our cook but, more importantly, our sharpshooter, especially from the top mast. Another man, Winston, from Jamaica, is our cannon expert. Abner Todd is my lookout. Other seamen are a Swahili warrior, Kondo, and two brothers who were Gloucester fishermen, Jason and Jonah Jackson."

Samuel smiled. "Sounds like a competent group, Captain Grant."

"My men call me Captain Pete, Samuel. As far as payment, Morgan's company gets 25 percent, as captain I get another 25 percent, and the crew shares the remaining half. Will that be sufficient?"

"I'm not doing this for the money," Samuel explained. "Whatever you pay everyone else is fine."

Morgan and Captain Pete looked at each other. "This is the type of man we've been looking for to round out the crew," Morgan said.

Samuel continued, "Would it be possible to have it put aside and forwarded to my family?"

"We do that for most of the men," Morgan said. "After each return to port, we'll give you a tally and have the funds sent wherever you ask. My staff will keep track of it for you. Anytime you come ashore, we can update you. We have a courier who can deliver the proceeds and any correspondence wherever you decide."

"Would your courier be able to return my horse to my family should I decide to go forward?" Samuel asked.

CHAPTER 29

"He'll be going into Massachusetts later in the week, and I can make sure of it for you. Leave any instructions and address with my office across from the docks. The storefront has a sign with 'MW Shipping' on the door, and I'll handle it for you," answered Morgan.

Samuel stared into his porridge for several minutes while the other men talked about a former Royal Navy raid in Falmouth. Samuel thought, *Forwarding any money I make and being able to send notes home that could possibly get to Lydia, I might be able to start setting us up for when I get tired of doing this.* Finally, he sat up, looked at the two men, and said, "All right, I'm ready. When do we start?"

Morgan slapped him on the back. "We're glad to have you. Ship sails from the pier on the edge of town first thing tomorrow."

"Welcome aboard, Mr. Prescott." The captain shook Samuel's hand. "See you at the crack of dawn."

Samuel left the two men talking alone. As he walked the streets of Portsmouth back to his inn, he looked up at the starlit sky; it reminded him again of Lydia. He thought to himself, *Maybe this is the opportunity to finally find my purpose and move closer to being with Lydia.* He thought about his discussions with Morgan and Captain Pete until he fell asleep that night, not knowing what was to come but looking forward to a new adventure.

PART 4

Conflict
Hardship
Resilience

CHAPTER 30

October 1776

Samuel arose early the next morning, anxious to begin this new phase of his life. First, he stopped at the Willis office and was told to bring Rascal to the stables owned by John Moffatt next to the Moffatt house along with his home address. He also left the courier a short note to give his father:

> *Father,*
>
> *I am sending Rascal back to you through this messenger. I'll be sending a packet occasionally from a man named Morgan Willis. It is payment I will be receiving for working at his enterprise. Please put it aside until I return, when I will explain all of this.*
> *Give my love to Mother, Benjamin, and Lucy.*
>
> *Samuel*

As he turned Rascal over to the stable boy, Samuel rested his head against the horse's muscular neck and patted him softly on the side of his head. Rascal snorted and stomped his right hoof on the ground several times, almost as if he knew what was happening. Samuel patted him once more then started walking to the docks. As he reached them, it was easy to pick out which ship was Captain

CHAPTER 30

Grant's. A sleek, two-masted schooner in front of him had a masthead carving with the head, wings and talons of an eagle but the body, rear legs, and tail of a lion—the mythical gryphon. The eagle's head was white and black, with a sharp, curved beak and piercing yellow eyes. The talons looked sharp and menacing while the black wings were open, creating the illusion it was prepared to fly away at any moment. The body and legs of the lion were dark brown. Samuel smiled, remembering what Captain Grant had said about the strength of the mythical creature and the protection of valuables that it represented; the figurehead symbolized it so well. The ship had originally been used to shuttle goods between Portsmouth and Boston but was apparently refitted with six cannons cut into the deck rails on each side.

Captain Grant was already onboard and yelled out his name, waving as he approached.

"Mr. Prescott, welcome aboard! Come meet your crew mates." The captain patted him on the back as Samuel walked up the gangplank and climbed onto the deck.

The men lined up at the captain's request, and each nodded to Samuel as Patrick, the first mate, introduced him. Bela was indeed the strongest man Samuel had ever met. When he was introduced to Kondo, the man smiled at him, saying, "Kondo is Swahili for war!" Abner Todd told Samuel that Captain Pete had let them know he was coming, and they were all pleased to have him join their ship.

After the introductions, Michael Ross took him below deck to see the mess area and sleeping quarters, explaining how the hammocks hanging between posts helped ease the swaying of the ship when they were sleeping. He pointed out the barrels of dried beef and salt pork they would be using to feed the crew, as well as dried peas, raisins, and fresh water. Michael also said several of the men were very skilled at catching some nice cod overboard. Samuel asked about fresh fruit, knowing it would be a necessity, and Michael told them they had some apples stored in the back.

He chuckled when Samuel asked about bananas. "No, Doc. Bananas are a bad curse on ships. You won't see any here."

Samuel spent the morning talking with each of the men, getting to know them as they prepared to depart. Afterward he met Captain Grant and Patrick back on deck.

"What do you think, Doc?" the captain asked.

"I'm glad to be here. Seems like a great group of men. I wasn't sure about the whole privateer concept, but my discussion last night with you and Morgan, and meeting your crew, has made me feel more comfortable."

The captain nodded. "Morgan is a great man, a man of honor and integrity who does what is right and proper. We're all privileged to work for him."

"We welcome you as part of our crew," Patrick added.

Soon Michael and Winston cast off the lines holding them to the dock while Patrick and Captain Pete manned the wheel. Several seagulls flew up from the water and circled around the ship, anticipating some scraps of food. Jason and Jonah hoisted the sails, Bela raised the anchor, and they slowly drifted downriver and out to sea. As they sailed away from the coast, Samuel took a deep breath of the fresh salt air and exhaled. He still had some doubts about his decision, but he was here now and wanted to make the best of it, especially if he could send some money home that could be forwarded to Lydia until his return. He watched quietly, deep in thought, as the rooftops and shoreline of Portsmouth slowly slipped away; the last image from the shore was the steeple of Portsmouth's North Church. He imagined John Moffatt watching them sail out of the harbor from an upper floor window of his lovely house. The captain steered the ship north, following the desolate, rocky coast of Maine. Samuel was amused at the many seals he saw on the numerous islands they passed as they sailed on the calm seas.

Chapter 31

Spring 1777

Samuel spent the first few months on board the *Gryphon* learning about seafaring life from other members of the crew. He often helped Michael with meal prep in the galley area. He had learned new knots from Jason and Jonah and showed them some of his medical skills by stitching some tears in the sails as needed. Samuel's skills also helped with the occasional rope burns, slivers from the wooden deck, and heat stroke when the men spent too long in the rigging. He watched for signs of scurvy from a lack of fresh fruit, such as swollen or bleeding gums or red spots on the shins of the men. One morning Samuel climbed to the crow's nest with Abner to get an idea of the vast view from that spot, and it reminded him of the many times he had climbed the tall oak trees at home with Abel as they were growing up. Adding to the excitement of the moment, Abner pointed out the fluke of a humpback whale off the starboard side of the ship. A few seconds later, the whale provided Samuel with the experience of a whale breaching, lifting itself above the calm water and splashing down again. Seeing such a splendid creature, as well as dolphins and the many seabirds, made all this seem like an adventure. Samuel was amazed at the spectacular sunrises out on the sea; they were unlike anything he had ever seen on shore.

When darkness fell on one cool spring night, Samuel laid back on the upper deck of the ship; the crisp April breeze felt refreshing. He stared at the wide, starlit sky. The sparkle and flickering of so many stars took him back to that large rock on the hill overlooking

Lexington two long years before. How he longed to be there again with Lydia. He pictured her looking up at the same sky. He could hear her soft, calming voice and feel her soft cheek against his face. Samuel tried to sleep, hoping to dream he was finally with her again, but was startled by Captain Grant. The captain had come up to the bow of the ship to sit with him. He had noticed Samuel liked to spend part of each evening there.

"Are you finally feeling better, Mr. Prescott? You had a couple of rough weeks getting acclimated to seafarer living." The captain seemed genuinely concerned.

"Yes, sir. The first week I was afraid of dying from the seasickness. The second week I actually hoped I would die. But eventually, I adjusted to being on the water."

The captain smiled and nodded. He looked out over the horizon for a few moments then spoke again to Samuel. "Doc, you always seem to be deep in thought when you're out here. I bet some young lady has your mind occupied."

"Yes, Captain. Left her one night two years ago and have wished I could have every minute of that time back. Don't know if you'd understand. Ever have a special woman in your life?"

"Aye, my young friend. A beautiful, elegant lass in Macchias. Stella Fairweather. A lovely lady who always made me feel like a king. Seriously considered giving up the seafaring life to marry her, but she knew my first love was being at sea and told me she would wait. I couldn't stay ashore. This is what I do. This is all I know. This is who I am. I couldn't be a farmer, tradesman, or shopkeeper. When all of this is done, maybe I will find something else to sustain me, but for now, the sea is my life. Hope some landlubber hasn't swept her away. I think we'll all be glad when this conflict is behind us."

After a moment of reflection and silence, Captain Grant continued, "I'm glad you decided to join us. This has been a good crew, but you have added some stability and a sense of calm for the men. Maybe it is knowing they have someone with medical knowledge onboard, or just your positive attitude and considerate demeanor. There is something comforting in your patience and daily presence. Your young lady will be lucky to have you."

CHAPTER 31

He leaned against the side rail, looking out over the calm ocean, then said, "Rest well tonight. I sense we will be busy soon enough. Now that the winter months have passed, sea traffic should increase." He said good night before returning to his quarters.

The next morning, Samuel had his first experience capturing a ship; it was simpler and less eventful than he had anticipated. A small sloop had grounded itself on a sand bar just outside the mouth of the Merrimack River off Plum Island and Newburyport. As the *Gryphon* approached, preparing for a fight from the vulnerable ship, the men on the other ship were waving their arms along the rail, some even holding white towels.

"Be careful, men," warned Captain Grant. "Could be a trap. Stay alert and have your guns and cutlasses ready."

When they pulled alongside the sloop, they discovered the ship was unarmed and only carried cargo, not weapons. The other crew did not resist capture, knowing they had nowhere to go with the ship stuck. Winston talked to them on their deck then returned to report to the Captain Pete.

"They are from the Caribbean, Captain," he explained. "They say they are carrying only food."

Captain Pete told Jonah and Jason to inspect the cargo hold. In a few minutes, they came on deck and yelled across to Captain Pete. "We found dozens of barrels of molasses, rum, and sugarcane. No weapons."

"Bring the cargo aboard. Let's see what happens when we reduce the weight," ordered Captain Grant.

Bela went down into the cargo hold and carried up the barrels one at a time. Because of their weight, though, it took two of the other men to move each of them onto the *Gryphon*. As expected, removing the many barrels allowed the sloop to rise off the sand bar to the cheers of the other ship's crew. Captain Grant put Patrick and the Jackson brothers onboard so they could accompany them back to Portsmouth. They turned in their bounty, released the crew of the other ship since they were harmless, and spent the night onshore. As was part of his routine, Samuel gathered some fruit, especially New England's bountiful apples, to have on board to prevent scurvy among the crew. First thing in the morning, they headed back out to sea.

As June arrived, the *Gryphon* crew expected more sea traffic as ships that had waited for better weather for crossing the Atlantic would be soon arriving. They were careful which ships would be targeted, avoiding convoys that usually included a few mighty and heavily armed man-of-war ships escorting the supply ships. An occasional straggler was an easy target. The effects of successful privateers were being felt by both sides, as the cargo seized was benefitting the war effort while the damage inflicted on the British supply chain had a larger impact than anything provided by the small and ineffective Continental Navy. The number of privateer ships soon outnumbered the ships commissioned for the Navy.

With the summer approaching, it also meant the occasional storm. Samuel had never thought about thunderstorms growing up in Concord. His room at their house was upstairs, so he had always found comfort from the rainfall on the roof and enjoyed the lightning flashing through the trees outside and the subsequent crack of thunder. But the storms at home paled in comparison to what he encountered at sea.

As a storm built on the horizon, the Jackson brothers dropped the sails. Captain Grant did his best to keep the bow of the ship facing into the wind and waves. Samuel could hear the moaning of the wooden hull as it crashed repeatedly against the stubbornly yielding waves. It was impossible to go on deck, between the listing of the ship from side to side, the gale force winds whipping across the deck, and the huge waves breaking over the rails. At times, the ship rose to the crest of a wave, and they could see all around them. Moments later, they dropped to the valley between waves, and the ocean surrounded them on all sides, almost swallowing the *Gryphon*. The normally blue water that sparkled in sunlight had turned an ominous black, dark and foreboding.

The thunder roared for over an hour with streaks of lightning flashing and illuminating the ocean surface around them. Rain blew sideways across the ship, feeling like the sting of dozens of bees on the faces of the captain and Patrick.

CHAPTER 31

And then it was over. As fast as it came, it passed, and the ocean slowly started to subside. The clouds cleared, the wind calmed, and the sails were raised again. They tried to get back on course and find another ship. As the seas calmed, Abner climbed into his crow's nest to watch for potential targets. Late in the afternoon, he spotted sails on the horizon, shouted down to the captain, and rang his alarm bell.

"Captain Pete! Starboard side ahead. Looks like a brig approaching."

The captain grabbed his spyglass as the men came on deck. Some armed themselves with muskets while the others manned the cannons. They all waited for orders.

"Looks like we have a good one, men. Decent-size brig, six cannons each side, same as us. We should be able to outmaneuver them and seize some treasure. Stay sharp."

Captain Grant sailed his ship toward the prize, eventually bringing the *Gryphon* alongside. As soon as they were parallel, the other ship fired two cannons in warning—one cannonball sailed over Samuel's head and splashed into the ocean on the other side while the second landed short, skipping and then falling into the sea.

"All right men, looks like they want a fight. Load and be ready on the two port side bow cannons. Wait for my order."

Bela and Winston manned one cannon while Michael and Kondo prepared the second. In a few moments, they received their order.

"Fire!" yelled Captain Grant.

Both cannons roared as they shot toward the other ship. Samuel saw one cannonball hit the side of the other ship just under the deck rail. The second splintered one of the foresail masts.

As soon as the cannons fired, Captain Grant turned the ship toward the other ship; but using the speed of the *Gryphon*, he passed in front of it before the enemy could get off another shot. As he crossed in front of the ship, he ordered the men to load again and fire, this time facing down the deck of the other ship. One cannonball took out two cannons on the starboard side while the second ripped off the deck railing on the port side.

Captain Pete then came around the other side of the ship; he ordered for the muskets to be loaded and fired as soon as they were within range. Two crew members of the other ship were hit and fell overboard. Captain Pete sailed the *Gryphon* past the ship and started to come back around on the other side.

"Captain, they're raising a white flag," yelled Abner. "They know they cannot outrace us or fight as well."

"Patrick, yell over to them we accept their surrender," Captain Pete said.

The men on the *Gryphon* cheered. They pulled alongside the brig, boarded it, and took control. As they accompanied it back to Portsmouth, they found it was carrying a hundred muskets, ten barrels of powder, and twenty barrels of musket balls—a nice bounty that would be very helpful to the Continental Army.

Over the next few months, they would make several trips to Portsmouth with captured ships; it also gave them a chance to restock the *Gryphon*. As each bounty was tallied and the crew was paid, Samuel had his shares sent home to Concord. He anticipated that another year aboard the ship would accumulate enough earnings for him to finally return home and reunite with Lydia.

Chapter 32

Summer 1777

Myles Latham had a heart as big as the rest of his body. His dedication and devotion to the Mulliken family helped them endure through many tough months. Since his commitment to Sam and Mrs. Mulliken when Sam enlisted, Myles had spent at least one day each week helping the family, whether tilling and cultivating their gardens, splitting and stacking firewood, repairing their well pump, or any endless number of household chores. But it was his boundless energy and spirit that gave them strength. His enthusiasm made even mundane chores seem manageable.

As summer came to an end, he kept a promise he had made earlier in the spring. While preparing the garden soils back in April, he told them he would have a celebration at the end of the summer.

"Mullikens, we have all worked so hard. We deserve a day to just enjoy our time together," he had said while resting on his tiller. "My wife, Prudence, will be celebrating her fiftieth birthday at the end of August. I'm inviting you all to share the moment with us."

"Thank you, Myles. That would be wonderful. You and Prudence have done so much for us," Mrs. Mulliken replied. "We can bring the many vegetables we harvest at that time of year to help you both celebrate. There hasn't been much to celebrate these past few years."

"Hah! We'll get a pork to roast from my neighbor and have a great day," the big man said.

The end of August came, and Myles asked them to come by the following Saturday. When they arrived, the roast pork he had promised was simmering on a spit in the fireplace. He had also provided a bottle of wine (a gift for his wife) and cider. The Mullikens brought potatoes, greens, carrots, and beans to add to the meal. Mary had made a bread, and they had fresh churned butter. They enjoyed a wonderful meal, and after eating, they presented Prudence with gifts.

First, Elijah Sanderson had dropped off a small cabinet for her to keep her candles and dry goods in. He was not able to stay but wished them all well. Mrs. Mulliken presented Prudence with a quilt she had made with help from Mary and Lydia. Joseph played her a tune on his fife to entertain her. Myles stood by, fidgeting, as he had something that he wanted to surprise her with.

He knelt before her, handing her a package wrapped in simple brown paper. He looked up at her and spoke softly.

"My dear Prudence. As you celebrate this special day with all of us, I wanted you to know it has been the greatest pleasure in my life to be your husband. All I ask is that we get to spend many, many more years together." He stood and kissed her on the cheek.

Prudence reached up and stroked his cheek as he pulled away. She unwrapped the paper on her lap and found a piece of fabric that had a heart embroidered in the center, with her initials on one side and Myles's initials on the other.

"Oh, Myles, this is beautiful. Where did you get this?" she asked, holding it up so they could all see it.

"Hah! My young friend, Rebeckah, made it for me when I asked her back in May. She was glad to help."

"Thank you, Rebeckah. And thank you all for making this day special for us."

After cleaning off the table, they all sat to relax quietly, the first time in many months there wasn't a lot of work to do. Lydia sat in an old rocker near the window with a cup of tea. Mary and the two younger children sat on the floor, drawing pictures for Prudence, who sat with Mrs. Mulliken near the fireplace. Myles was leaning against the wall, eating a piece of apple pie that his wife had baked for him. As Lydia smiled at him, she noticed a yellow pamphlet on

CHAPTER 32

top of some worn books on the windowsill, with the words "The American Crisis."

"Myles, what is that document next to you?" she asked.

"Oh, something I picked up in town. It was posted with town notices, and there were several copies. I saw it had been written by a man named Thomas Paine, who printed an essay I enjoyed called 'Common Sense' a year ago, and I wanted to see what he had written."

"May I look at it?" Lydia asked.

"Of course." Myles took it off the windowsill and gave it to her.

Lydia leaned over near a candle to see it better and started to read:

> *These are times that try men's souls; the summer soldier and sunshine patriot will, in this crisis, shrink from the services of his country; but he that stands it now, deserves the love and thanks of man and woman. Tyranny, like hell, is not easily conquered; yet we have this consolation with us, that the harder the conflict, the more glorious the triumph. What we obtain too cheap, we esteem too lightly.*

Lydia put it down. "Inspirational words, but times that try *men's* souls? Seriously? What about women's souls? I respect and appreciate the sacrifice of the men fighting for our liberty, but those of us battling every day to just survive have had trying times as well."

Prudence nodded and said, "I believe Mr. Paine referred to 'men' as in mankind. But you're right. We women have fought to maintain our freedoms as well, even if we aren't soldiers."

Myles spoke up. "Lydia, you will appreciate the discussion I heard while dropping off some buckles for Jeremiah at the Fitch Tavern in Bedford last week. Apparently, the women up in Pepperell took matters into their own hands. A woman named Prudence, coincidentally," he said, smiling at his wife, "Prudence Wright, as I recall, organized a group of women to guard their town. Her brothers were staunch supporters of the Crown, but she and her husband, David, were fierce patriots. When David led a group of the men out of town to respond to the Lexington and Concord alarm, Prudence gathered the women to patrol Pepperell, armed with pitchforks, spears, and just a few muskets. At one point, they seized a Loyalist courier from New Hampshire who was trying to cross a bridge in town, bringing him to Groton to be kept captive. One of Prudence's brothers saw her from across the bridge as the group of men approached, turned quickly, and galloped back to New Hampshire."

"If I saw one of my sisters in that situation, I would do the same thing, but really fast," mumbled Joseph, sitting on the floor. They all laughed.

"Don't worry, Joseph," his mother replied. "None of my daughters are becoming soldiers. I already have too many sons fighting for this glorious cause."

"Hah! Good thing, Joseph," said Myles. "We would have been vastly outnumbered here."

They spent the rest of the evening enjoying each other's company. Despite the many hardships, loneliness and worry for loved ones, being able to be together helped each of them cope with their feelings and worries, giving them hope for better days ahead.

Chapter 33

Fall 1777

"Captain Pete! Ship ahead!" shouted Abner from the crow's nest one fall morning.

The crew all came on deck to see if they could get a view of the ship, looking to see if it was friend or enemy.

Captain Grant yelled up to Abner, "What flag is it flying?"

Abner lifted his spyglass and replied, "It looks like the Union Jack."

Captain Grant went to the front of the ship with his own spyglass to get a better look. "Wait a minute," he said. "That ship looks familiar."

He waited until they were a little closer and let out a loud laugh. "No worries, men. At ease." Then he yelled out, "Augustine Scott, you rascal! I'll be damned."

The crew looked at each other, not understanding what was happening. The captain let the ship draw alongside, and he shouted across to the captain on the other ship, "You cod-faced bottom dweller!"

The other captain, standing along the front rail, yelled back, "You smell like a rotten squid, even from this distance!" Both men laughed loudly.

As the ships drifted next to each other, a gangplank was placed between them, and they were lashed together so the other captain could board the *Gryphon*.

"Pete," he said warmly, "so great to see you."

"My friend, Augie, what are you doing flying a damn British flag?" asked Captain Grant.

"Decoy—best way to be safe out here. The Royal Navy ignores me until I get close enough to attack, and most of the Continental Navy just avoids me."

"You fool. I could have blown you out of the water if I hadn't recognized that floating wreck you call a ship. I'm always on the watch for Henry Mowat, that Royal Navy villain who has been wreaking havoc along the Maine coast. I would love to get revenge for him attacking and burning Falmouth back in '75."

"Lucky for you, it was just me!"

"You named your ship the *Angry Unicorn*. What happened to the figurehead?" Grant said, pointing at the front of the other ship.

"Ahh, I was trying to dock in Camden Harbor during a storm and kind of bumped another ship. Broke off the horn of my unicorn."

"Looks more like a timid pony now. You'll have to rename it." They laughed.

"You know it is unlucky to rename a ship," Augie said.

They put their arms around each other as they crossed the deck. "Men, this is Augie Scott, a longtime friend. We go way back," Captain Pete explained.

Captain Scott smiled at the crew. "We started as lobstermen and had many adventures together."

"Oh, sure we did, like the time we started that brawl in the bar in York Harbor," said Captain Grant.

"That was all your fault. I just wanted to relax with some mead and a block of cheese," insisted Augie.

"Yes, until you started going after the barmaid, who was the owner's daughter!"

"What about the time you dropped anchor so we could pull up traps and you forgot it wasn't tied to the ship?" asked Augie.

"We needed a new anchor anyways," answered Grant.

The men on board laughed at their many stories. Captain Scott had his crew roll a barrel of rum over the gangplank from the *Angry Unicorn* so the crews could share, the two ships slowly drifting on the calm ocean waves. The two crews spent a few hours together,

CHAPTER 33

listening to the two captains share memories. Eventually, the crews separated. The two friends wished each other well, and the *Angry Unicorn* sailed away.

Later that week, the pleasantries were quickly forgotten. The surroundings at sea were often very unpredictable, and this day was one of them. A perfectly beautiful, clear day could change drastically as a fog bank could close in out of nowhere. Such was the weather one fall day as the *Gryphon* sailed off the coast of Maine. Like a ghost ship drifting aimlessly wrapped in a heavy blanket of fog, the ship patiently waited for the fog to clear. The men kept ready to follow any orders from their captain once the weather cleared; Michael and Samuel worked in the mess below, preparing the next meal. Captain Grant ordered the sails lowered so they could ride out the fog, occasionally ringing the deck bell as a warning to other ships nearby. They had been away from Portsmouth for a while without seeing another ship, but were always on the alert for potential targets.

Suddenly, without warning, a massive ship came out of the fog in front of them. A man-of-war, with three tall masts and almost seventy cannons on board bore down on them quickly. The men of the *Gryphon* hurried to raise sail, grab their weapons, and prepare for a fight. Bela moved several barrels of powder closer to the cannons while Kondo loaded muskets. Captain Grant was able to move his ship just in time before the two ships would have collided, but the surprise enabled the larger ship to have an advantage.

Captain Grant tried to gain a better fighting position, but the light breeze made it difficult. Before he could get turned, several of the larger ship's cannons exploded with fire. The second mast of the *Gryphon* shattered and fell onto the deck, crushing Kondo before he could move. Another cannon blast smashed into the masthead, blowing off the head and wings of the *Gryphon* carving. As Bela was trying to load a cannon, he was hit in the chest with a cannon ball from the other ship; it threw him back against the rail, killing him instantly. Michael was able to get off a musket shot and appeared to hit one of the crew members on the other ship, but it wasn't enough. Another round of cannon fire pounded the hull of the *Gryphon*, creating a gaping hole just above water level. Several of the sailors on the other ship shot burning arrows into her remaining sails, catching them on fire. Winston was blown off the ship as a cannonball from the enemy hit one of the barrels of powder he was moving. When it exploded, he was thrown from the deck and was lost at sea.

Samuel tried to help Jason and Jonah get one of the cannons that were facing the larger ship loaded; they were under constant fire from muskets alongside. They struggled to move among the rigging and pieces of the second mast that had fallen on deck. It became impossible to stand on the deck without being hit by fire from the other ship. Pieces of burning canvas from the sails on the main mast were falling around them like large, fiery snowflakes. Jason and Jonah were able to fire one cannon toward the larger ship, hitting a small boat alongside that was being launched for a boarding party, throwing its passengers into the ocean. Michael fired his musket again, striking another man along the other ship's rail, who fell overboard. But the crew of the *Gryphon* could not maintain the same level of fire as what was incoming from the large man-of-war. Captain Grant continued to try to move his ship to a safer position, but it was useless.

"Men, I am going to try to ram them if I can get control of our ship. Be prepared," he shouted to what was left of his crew. He turned the wheel of the *Gryphon* to guide her toward the larger ship, but with only the one mast left, his ship didn't respond. Patrick went to the stern to see if the rudder was working and was hit by musket fire, falling off the rear of the ship.

Soon it was obvious the battle was over; the *Gryphon* crew was overmatched and outgunned. Boarding parties from the larger ship started to come onboard, armed with pistols and cutlasses. Michael tried to fight off several of the attackers but was slashed by one of their swords and fell to the ground; he was then stabbed. Samuel ran to help him but was grabbed on each side by men behind him, and he was tackled to the ground; his hands and feet were tied. The remaining men of the *Gryphon* never had a chance and surrendered. They were transported back to the larger ship, shackled, and thrown into the cargo hold. As they started below deck, they saw the remains of the *Gryphon* engulfed in flames as the last boarding party poured oil onto her deck and set her on fire.

Chapter 34

Fall 1777

The sail from just off the Maine Coast to Nova Scotia was uneventful and relatively smooth for the new captives, except for the discomfort of being in shackles and down in the dark, cold hull. Jason and Jonah were glad they were still together. Abner was frightened, not sure what was going to happen to them. Captain Grant told them to be calm.

Samuel tried to reassure them all. "We'll make the best of this. Let's see what's in store for us, then we can decide what to do next."

Approaching Halifax, Samuel saw the remains of what had been a large British ship floating a short distance off the coast. It was almost unrecognizable—just a dark wooden hull, with masts, rigging, and deck structures removed. Holes had been cut into the sides of the hull like small windows to provide a small amount of fresh air. When the crew of the *Gryphon* was rowed out to the prison ship, they were stunned at the conditions. The men who were already there were sick, looked like living skeletons, and the stench was overwhelming. There were lice evident on many of the men, and flies were everywhere. Occasionally, mice or roaches could be seen scurrying along the floor. Body odors, the bitter smell of urine, and the unmistakable scent of disease made several of the men sick as they were pushed down into the bowels of the old ship. They had nothing but boxes and a few old blankets to sit or sleep on, and many of the men there had very little clothing left. There were old wooden buckets for them to use as needed.

At mealtime, things were even worse. They were given dried, uncooked meat, peas, and old, moldy bread. Some of the meat had maggots crawling over it. The water that was dropped down into the hull was rancid and dirty, sometimes in the same old wooden buckets they used for other functions.

On the first morning, they were "welcomed" by Commander Clark Morris, a former Royal Navy officer who had been moved to Halifax to monitor the prisoner situation. He was a tall, thin man, with a black goatee and bushy black eyebrows; his nose was long, pointed, and slightly crooked.

"You men are now here at my mercy," he began. "You will follow the orders of the guards. We will allow you to have an hour on deck each day to walk and exercise, but you can only congregate in groups of four or five."

He walked in front of the line of men, his hands clutched behind his back. "I strongly suggest that you volunteer for service in the Royal Navy rather than remain here. Which of you is Captain Grant?"

Captain Pete stepped forward. "I'm Grant," he said.

"Take him away," Commander Morris ordered to the guards. "Your reputation as a ship captain precedes you, and we need your experience. You're being sent to New York to command one of our vessels."

"No thanks. I'm staying here," said Captain Pete, stepping back into the group of prisoners.

"That wasn't a request, Grant." The commander motioned with his head and two of the guards grabbed Captain Pete, taking him away.

"The rest of you are expected to follow orders. I may grant some extra food or listen to complaints from those who cooperate or are willing to help fellow prisoners."

Samuel spoke up. "Sir, these are not safe conditions for these men. Can we get some fresh water, maybe some clean linens?"

The commander walked up to Samuel, his face inches from Samuel's. "And just who are you?" the commander asked.

"Dr. Samuel Prescott, proud Concord resident."

CHAPTER 34

"A doctor? Oh, good. You can be responsible for helping these sick men so I don't have to risk my own men. If you behave, I may listen to your requests. Guards, put them back in the hold."

In the first few days, it was obvious to Samuel this was a dangerous situation. He spotted signs of scurvy among the prisoners, as they were losing teeth and had reddish blue welts on their legs. Under these terrible conditions, it was not surprising for seven to eight men to die each day. The conditions in prisons/prison ships for prisoners of war were deplorable enough without the additional issue of overcrowding. Both sides in the conflict had the same problem—capturing the enemy without sufficient shelters and resources to provide for them. To alleviate this, prisoners were sometimes given the choice to join the British Navy or Army. Another solution was an occasional prisoner swap negotiated between sides.

A month after the *Gryphon* crew was added to the prison population, Commander Morris welcomed the opportunity to exchange fifty of his prisoners for fifty British soldiers, expecting he could then transfer the men back to the military. Morris polled his guards for a list of the men they felt should be part of the exchange. Because of Samuel's continued cooperation and ability to assist in caring for others, he was included on the list as a measure of the guards' approval and appreciation.

On the day of the exchange, the guards rounded up their selections and brought them on deck. They were somewhat confused, but having seen exchanges before, some were hopeful as well. As the sentries who had suggested Samuel approached him to let him know it was his turn, he surprised them by declining.

"Absolutely not," he said. "There are several men here who are much older than I am, many who have been here much longer, and most are in much worse health. Choose one of them instead. I will wait my turn."

"But you have earned this opportunity to leave. Are you sure?" asked one of the guards.

"Yes. I'm not going at this time. But tell Commander Morris I want to speak with him as he promised."

The guard shrugged and took one of the other men in Samuel's place.

The next day, the guard informed Samuel he had been granted time with the commander. Later that morning, when the prisoners were brought up for their daily hour long walk on deck, Samuel was taken for the meeting with Commander Morris. As the other prisoners were returned to the cargo hold, Samuel was shackled, put in a small boat with two of the guards, and rowed ashore to the seaside home occupied by the commander.

Samuel was led inside by one of the guards. Commander Morris was sitting behind a large oak desk. A fireplace on the side wall made the room warm. Samuel was told by the guard to stand in front of the desk. The commander looked up at him and spoke.

"I understand you wanted to speak with me. What is this about?" He leaned back in his chair, holding a red apple in his left hand and a dagger in his right hand.

"You had said I could speak to you about conditions below deck. I have some concerns regarding the hazards to the health of my fellow prisoners."

Morris rolled his eyes then leaned forward. "Is that so? What do you suggest be done?"

"As a doctor, I find the sanitation and food issues extremely unhealthy. I have some ideas I thought you would find easy to implement."

Morris stared at him for several moments, then yelled out to his aide in the other room, "Abernathy! Get in here! Bring a quill and paper. I need to record what this man wants done."

A short, slightly overweight man stumbled into the room and sat at a small table along the wall.

"All right, Prescott. What ideas do you have for me to consider?" The commander sat back again, peeling the apple slowly with the dagger, putting a piece in his mouth, and looking up at Samuel.

"Well, first, I think we need fresh fruit, like the apple you have there. We don't get enough fresh fruits or vegetables."

CHAPTER 34

"Did you get that, Abernathy? More fresh fruits and vegetables? Here in Nova Scotia, during a war?" He shook his head and gestured at Samuel to continue.

"The water we receive is delivered in the same buckets used to remove waste from the prisoners. Can you at least provide clean buckets used only for water and nothing else?"

The commander looked at Samuel, as though he was contemplating this idea, then said, "What else?"

"I am glad to assist with the care of the men here but need some supplies, especially medications. Are there any available through your underused commissary?"

"Nope, sorry. You are on your own. Next." He put another piece of apple in his mouth.

"Fresh linens more often. Those we have are old, torn, dirty."

The commander snickered then said, "Go on!"

"One hour each morning to walk on deck is not sufficient. We need more sunlight, and the men have to get more exercise. Can we have a second hour, maybe before evening?"

The commander leaned toward his desk and slammed the dagger into the wooden top. His face was flushed, and his teeth clenched. He stood up and shouted at Samuel, "Enough, now. You've had your chance to speak. Guard, return him to the ship."

The guard grabbed Samuel's arm and pulled him outside. They walked to the small boat where the other guard was waiting, and he was rowed back to the prison ship.

Morris took the paper Abernathy had been using for notes, walked to the fireplace, and threw the paper inside. "Damn fool. He should have stayed in Concord, treating the common maladies of the old wenches in town." The paper slowly curled, the edges darkened, then it ignited. "Abernathy, get me a glass of wine," the commander ordered. The aide scurried off to complete the task.

When Samuel returned to the ship, his former crewmates asked him what had happened.

"I told him what we needed, but we'll see if anything gets done," Samuel replied.

Abner shook his head. "I don't believe anything will get done. We need to take care of this situation ourselves."

One night the following week, Jason and Jonah came to sit next to Samuel, looking over their shoulders and speaking to him in a whisper.

"Doc, we think we know how to get out of here," Jason said.

Jonah spoke after his brother. "We're going to try to escape, but want you to join us."

Abner also joined their discussion. "I know the shipping schedules from helping Captain Pete for so long. In a day or two, there will be several privateers just off shore. If we can get away from here and find some refuge down the coast, we can get picked up and be done with this pit of a place."

"But how?" Samuel asked. "We're under constant guard."

Jason looked around and spoke up. "The old, overweight guard they have here at night usually falls asleep just before dawn. If we time it right, Doc, we can sneak past him, cross the deck before sunrise, and jump overboard."

"You can't swim that far in the cold water here, especially this late in the season," Samuel said.

"During our daily walks, we have been able to loosen some of the boards on deck. We should be able to pull them up before we jump, using them to float on if needed," Jonah replied. "We would really like you to come with us."

"Be very careful," he warned them. "If you don't make it, you will probably be killed. I want to be out of here as much as any of you, but that is much too dangerous."

"Understood," Jason nodded. "But we are going to try tomorrow night."

"Thank you for all you've done for us since joining our crew," Abner said.

"I'll do anything I can to protect you as you make your move. God be with you," Samuel told them.

The next night, Samuel saw the three men slowly gather at the bottom of the wooden stairway to the deck, looking up at the guard. As the night wore on, they saw the man start to yawn and sit on a

CHAPTER 34

bench at the top of the stairs. As soon as they were sure he was dozing, they made their move.

Samuel went to stand nearby in case they needed a distraction. As the three men reached the deck, he saw the guard's head snap up, realizing he had fallen asleep. Before the guard could see the three men crawling along the deck, Samuel yelled up to him.

"Hey, mate, we haven't had any water all day. Can you get us a bucket?" Samuel shouted.

"Go back to sleep! Water won't be here until morning," the guard yelled back. Then he heard the snapping of some of the boards that the three former *Gryphon* crew members were breaking loose across the deck.

"Halt! Prisoners loose!" he screamed, grabbing his musket and running to the side of the old ship.

Samuel heard the splashes as the three men jumped overboard. He went to one of the window vents on the seaward side of the hull to see if he could locate them. Through the very pale early morning light, he could barely make them out as they swam or floated away. Above, several other guards could be heard running along the deck, and soon shots were ringing out. Several more prisoners, wakened by the noise above them, rushed to the window vents to see what was happening. Samuel saw one of the men in the water trying to swim, apparently without a plank. He was hit in the back by a musket ball, shuddered as he was struck, then floated motionless in the water. Samuel saw another man who he recognized as Jonah, laying on a board and paddling as hard as he could away from the ship, but he was also hit by musket fire, rolling off the board, struggling for an instant, then also floating still. Samuel could not see the third man, and the firing had stopped, so he hoped one of them had actually made it away safely. The guards came down into the hold to get everyone away from the windows and quiet them down. Many of them talked all day about what had happened.

The next morning, all the captives were assembled on deck. Commander Morris walked along in front of them, his hands behind his back.

"We had an incident early yesterday. The guard involved has been disciplined and removed from his service. If I hear of any other attempts to escape, or even hear of discussions regarding the same, the guilty parties will be hung from the rear of the ship. And I'll do all in my power to prevent any further prisoner exchanges going forward. Your daily breaks to walk on deck have been suspended for a week."

One of the other prisoners had been pulled aside, with shackles placed on his hands and feet. A large metal bar was added to the chains on his feet. He was taken to the side of the deck. "Let this be a warning and example to all of you," the commander shouted. The man was then thrown overboard to the shock of everyone present.

The commander excused all the prisoners, ordering the guards to get them back below deck. As they started to move, he turned and yelled back at them, "And, by the way, a third body washed up on shore nearby this morning. The third escapee apparently drowned before he got too far." He turned, grinning at one of the guards, and returned to his quarters.

Three weeks later, another group of recent captives arrived at the prison. A young man with curly red hair was put into the area near Samuel. He looked frightened and confused, trembling as he was put into the hold, not knowing where to go. Samuel introduced himself and tried to reassure him.

"I'm Samuel Prescott. I'm sorry you have been added to our group in this horrid situation, but we'll try to help you adjust to the conditions and make you as comfortable as possible."

"Thank you, Mr. Prescott. I'm Jacob Winter. We were marching through New Hampshire on the way to help with the campaign in Canada when we were captured."

"Where are you from, Jacob?" Samuel asked. "And please, call me Samuel."

"Ashburnham, Massachusetts, Samuel. A small village in the north central part of the colony."

"Yes, I know where it is. I'm from Concord."

"Really? How did you end up here?"

CHAPTER 34

"Captured while on a privateer off the coast, trying to intercept weapons and supplies."

They talked long into the night, and over the next few weeks, they became good friends. They would talk for hours at a time, day and night, trying to ignore the constant hunger. Of course, food often crept into the conversations. Jacob would recall a favorite bakery he used to visit in Winchendon, hunting in southern New Hampshire, or a sleighride through the fields of Westminster. Samuel told him stories of swimming and fishing in the Concord River with his brothers, meeting friends at Wright's Tavern, or picking apples at an orchard in Carlisle. And there was always some type of reference to his dear Lydia.

Day after long day and sleepless, restless nights turned to weeks and months. Jacob saw his friend slowly declining; he tried to use memories of Lydia to help Samuel focus and fight for strength. Even occasional visits from local citizens, bearing gifts such as fresh produce from gardens or sacks of potatoes didn't generate interest from Samuel. Samuel had requested two more meetings with the commander that had been refused.

Samuel himself felt his health failing. As his health deteriorated, images flashed across his mind between occasional losses of consciousness. He could see the house in Concord and hear his father's voice, see himself swimming in the Concord River with his brothers. He could almost feel Duchess under him, as she galloped so quickly across the fields in town. Meanwhile, the hunger tore at his insides as he thought of meeting friends with Abel at Wrights Tavern. Memories of his work during the siege of Boston and at Ticonderoga filled his thoughts, and doubt still remained about his decision to go to sea. Samuel was saddened by thoughts of losing his brother, Abel, and close friend, William Emerson. Yet a faint smile reached his dried, parched lips. He was remembering Lydia and their picnic in Concord and the night at her house when he left, seeing her sliding the purple ribbon from her chestnut hair, which fell and cascaded over her shoulders. He could almost smell the fragrance of lavender over the stench he had become accustomed to during his wretched time here. Visions of her and her smile flooded his brain. Samuel opened his eyes to see if she was really there. He could see up through the hatch door as it was opened to throw down some water. It was the dead of night, and there, just above him, he could faintly see stars flickering in the clear, dark sky. Somewhere, maybe *she* was looking at the sky now too. As Samuel's eyes slowly closed, he could picture Lydia leaning over to kiss him like she had on that flat stone on the hill so long ago. It was the last image in his mind as he drifted away for the last, permanent time.

Dawn was welcomed with a gray, steely sky, depositing a soft, cold drizzle on those below. During the morning, Jacob let the guards know that Samuel was gone. They removed his body along with several others. He was wrapped in a sheet and taken ashore with the other unfortunate souls who had finally found peace. They were buried together in an unmarked common grave along the shore of the bay outside Halifax.

Chapter 35

January–September 1778

The Blizzard of '78 started as just a dusting, with light snow coating the bare ground during the early part of the day. It had been a warmer than usual winter, but as late January approached, the skies became more ominous.

By evening, the wind picked up, howling angrily, shaking the walls of the house and rattling the windows. The wind whistled as it found cracks in the walls or edge of windows, depositing some snowflakes along the sides of the windows. The candles that Mary lit for some light flickered and danced from the draft.

Mrs. Mulliken had Mary and Lydia collect all the quilts and blankets from throughout the house. They gathered them in front of the fireplace, and the family huddled together to try to ride out the storm, hoping it would pass by morning. Joseph had gathered some additional firewood and stored it in the back room, but it was being consumed quickly by the roaring fire needed to keep them warm. An occasional downdraft in the chimney caused by the fierce wind would smother the flame for an instant then blow smoke and some ash into the room. Rebeckah choked on some of the smoke until she could catch her breath. After nightfall, in the dark and bitter cold, they did all they could to stay warm. They could hear the cracking of trees outside as large branches were pulled off by the ferocious wind. Throughout the night, they listened to the howling winds over the crackling of the slowly fading fire.

After a very cold and restless night, the Mullikens woke to a calming sunrise. The storm had finally passed. Joseph went to the window to look outside; he saw the glistening icicles that were hanging from the roof being warmed by a rising sun. A droplet of melting snow slowly trickled down the length of one of the large icicles, pausing at the tip where it slowly grew until it dripped off into the deep white snow below. The white birch trees seen through that window had bent over from the weight of the wet, sticky snow on their branches, creating a magical arch. A tall blue spruce sparkled with the needles frosted with snow crystals.

The warmth from the fireplace was slowly diminishing as they had used most of the wood. Mary opened the front door to find that a snowdrift had filled the entire doorway; a pile of soft snow fell at her feet.

"Dear Lord, how will we get out to get more wood?" she asked to no one in particular.

Rebeckah went to the back door and found that it was also nearly blocked with snow.

"We'll have to wait for some of it to melt and hope someone comes by," their mother said, worried that it could be a while.

"I can try to get out, Mother," Joseph offered. "I know where the woodpile is and should be able to dig myself through the snow."

"No, Joseph, the drifts are too high. You'll get buried in one of them, and we wouldn't be able to come and get you out," Lydia explained.

"But my toes and fingers are already numb," said Rebeckah, blowing on her hands and rubbing them on her skirt.

Mrs. Mulliken wrapped Rebeckah in one of the many blankets and quilts they had used to huddle together overnight. All of them sat in front of the fireplace as close as possible to the few remaining embers, taking in whatever warmth was being provided.

About an hour later, as they shivered together, Lydia stood up, thinking she heard something outside. Suddenly there was a knock at the door.

"Mullikens, are you in there?" It sounded like Myles.

CHAPTER 35

Joseph ran to the door and opened it to a strange sight—standing there, covered in snow and looking even more like a mountain, was Myles Latham.

"Hah! My friend Joseph. How are you?"

"Cold!" Joseph said.

"Myles, how did you ever get here?" asked Mrs. Mulliken.

"I came over the snow on snowshoes with these other men to check on you. We have shovels and will clear the doorways and woodpile for you."

Looking outside, Mary saw Elijah and another man helping Myles. The men spent the next two hours removing snow from the doors and walkways, creating snowbanks that were more than shoulder height. When the back of the house was completed, Myles and one of the other men came in with their arms full of firewood, which they used to build a roaring fire in a few minutes; it added refreshing heat to the room.

Myles shook snow off his coat, smiling at all of them. "Mrs. Mulliken, our friend, Elijah, had come to me to suggest we check on you when the storm first started. This other gentleman, Joseph Burrill, was staying with Prudence and me. He provides me with my leather aprons and gloves from his tannery in Haverhill. Guess he picked a bad day to travel, as he had just arrived when the storm rolled in. Hah! Luckily, he also makes snowshoes!"

"Gentlemen, thank you all so very much. We don't know what we would have done." Mrs. Mulliken nodded to each of them as they removed their wool hats and bowed in return.

"Let us make you something while you dry off and warm up," Lydia suggested.

"No, Prudence has been baking all day, so there would be plenty to eat when we returned with healthy appetites," said Myles. "It'll take us a while to snowshoe back, and we want to get there before dark. But thank you."

The men gathered their shovels, strapped on their snowshoes, waved, and left. As they disappeared over the snow-white horizon, the Mullikens heard a familiar "Hah!"

Winter passed. One late April day, a spring sun forced its way into the early morning sky. The first rays entered Lydia's room and woke her. She turned, looking out her window at a cloudless sky. She briefly reclosed her eyes, imagining Samuel riding up to the house on his horse, smiling broadly as he saw her waiting in the door. The sharp pain of that image opened her eyes wide. How she ached whenever her mind pictured him! The wrenching heartache, so intense and painful, was there with every thought of him. The knot in her stomach, the lump in her throat, the tears welling in her eyes—each time seemed stronger and more agonizing. How many seasons had passed since her last moments with Samuel? She had lost track of the winter snows, the flowers blooming in spring, and the hot summers since that last night. She missed him terribly.

The noise of activity in the kitchen helped her once again subdue the despair and loneliness. Her responsibilities to her family, especially the youngest children, forced her to focus and disregard her pain. Only in moments of solitude could she allow herself to dwell on the misery of her missing love. After dressing, Lydia went to the kitchen to help with the daily routine. At least the everyday chores provided some distraction; her love of her mother, brother, and sisters also helped alleviate any sadness inside.

Summer came, and life went on while hope remained for change. Outside Lydia heard the chattering of a pair of chickadees hopping between branches in a tree. It made her smile. But the smile faded when her mother shared troubling news from some former neighbors. Apparently, people throughout the colony were dealing with the struggle of disease in their families. It had become as much of a burden as the fight for independence. Smallpox, dysentery, and other terrible diseases had flourished in the Cambridge area and taken a toll on so many families. They could only hope it wouldn't affect them.

However, in late August, the Mullikens found out that young Moses Childs, born just after the April 1775, raid by the Regulars, had died at only three years old. That tragedy was followed four days later when his twelve-year-old sister, Eunice, also died. She was followed by four-year-old Benjamin, thirteen-year-old Sarah, and sev-

CHAPTER 35

en-year-old Abigail by the end of the month. In early September, eleven-year-old Abyah suffered the same fate, leaving Sarah Childs and her husband, Abijah, close friends of the Mullikens, with only their one-year-old infant, Isaac, who somehow survived. Their six children had died within eighteen days of each other; they were buried a few feet from Nathaniel in Lexington's Old Burial Ground.

Up to that point, the Mullikens had been spared. However, their good fortune changed when both Rebeckah and Joseph fell ill. Their illness started with a slight fever, then lethargy, and loss of appetite. When a few sores started to show on Rebeckah's arms, Mrs. Mulliken became very concerned.

They all wished Samuel was around, as his medical knowledge was needed; also, the children were comfortable around him. Since Samuel wasn't available, Myles was able to get them in touch with Prudence's doctor, who was glad to assist.

The doctor examined both Rebeckah and Joseph and instructed their mother and older sisters, "Do all you can to go near them only when absolutely necessary, such as for feeding or cleaning. The pox is very contagious. Watch the sores. As long as those don't start to blister, the children have a chance." He told Mrs. Mulliken and her two oldest daughters to keep the sick children as comfortable as possible and he would check back in a few days.

The next day, the vomiting and diarrhea worsened for Joseph, but Rebeckah seemed to be slightly better. Mary and Lydia took turns placing cool, damp cloths on their foreheads and bringing them water and bread or biscuits, doing all they could to avoid breathing the same air and keeping contact to a minimum. Lydia, Mary, and their mother spent many sleepless nights trying to keep the youngest members of the family comfortable and praying they would survive.

A week later, the doctor returned. He was relieved that Rebeckah's sores had gone away; her vomiting and diarrhea had subsided as well, but she still had a headache. His concern for Joseph, however, was deepened by the boy's worsening condition. Myles had also come by to see how they were doing and felt terribly about the boy. He brought some food and supplies but kept his distance, fearing bringing the disease back to Prudence.

In a couple of days, Rebeckah started eating more, the headache and upset stomach went away, and she seemed to be on the road to recovery.

At supper, Mrs. Mulliken told Mary and Lydia, "It looks like we were able to get Rebeckah on track, but I'm not sure about Joseph."

"His symptoms keep getting worse, and he won't eat," Mary said.

"We have to watch him carefully," added Lydia.

During one long, restless night a week later, Lydia was startled by noises coming from Joseph's room. She wrapped a shawl around her shoulders, brought a cloth to cover her mouth, and went to his door. She had to listen more closely as she thought she heard music. Lydia slowly opened the door, and she was surprised to see Joseph sitting on his bed, playing his fife!

"Joseph! Are you feeling better?" she asked, surprised at the sight.

"Lydia, can I have some of the porridge you made yesterday? I'm very hungry."

"Of course, my dear, sweet brother," Lydia said, then called out to her mother and Mary. "Mother, Mary, come see Joseph." Lydia wrapped her arms around him, joined a few minutes later by Mary and their mother. They first cried then celebrated with a large bowl of porridge for Joseph.

As he devoured the food, Joseph looked up at his mother. "I hope I made this one of those good days for you."

"Oh, yes, son. It is a very good day."

They were among the lucky few who had to deal with the disease running rampant through the colony without losing one of the children. For once, they had been spared another tragedy. This time, it appeared misfortune passed them by. They prayed it would continue.

Chapter 36

October 1778

Time has a way of passing quickly when the hard work of daily chores fills the days. More than two years had passed since Nathaniel's death, and the Mullikens continued to do the best they could to sustain a somewhat-normal life. As summer and the heat and humidity faded into the cooler autumn, Lydia was outside gathering some lavender and sage from their garden. She looked up and saw a bright red cardinal and his mate fluttering and chirping among branches of the trees nearby. Once again, she wished her own "mate" was there.

Her thoughts were interrupted by the sound of a single rider coming up the road toward her. For an instant, her heart raced. Could it be Samuel? Was he really finally home? The brief rush of adrenaline sadly faded as the man on the horse came closer, and she was able to get a better look at him. He appeared to be younger than her, pale, and extremely thin, almost sickly.

The man stopped in front of her and asked, "Excuse me, madam. Would you by any chance know where I can find the Mulliken family?"

Stunned, Lydia responded, "Why, yes, sir. I'm one of the Mullikens."

"I'm looking for a Miss Lydia. A very nice woman in town told me I might find Lydia here."

"Kind sir, you have found her. I'm Lydia."

The man seemed to turn even paler. He dismounted from his horse, grimacing with every move and slowly removed his hat, exposing thinning red hair; he reached out his hands to take hers.

"Lydia, my name is Jacob Winter. I'm on my way home to Ashburnham, but I wanted to desperately find the young lady I've heard so much about for months."

"Go on," Lydia said, curious what this was all about.

"I've recently been released from a dark and terrible prison ship in Nova Scotia as part of a prisoner exchange. While I was there, I spent a great deal of time with a Dr. Samuel Prescott."

Lydia's hand went to her mouth, and she had to lean back against the stone wall. She suddenly felt a knot in her stomach.

"All he talked about was you," Jacob went on. "I've never known anyone so devoted and so focused on being with another person as he was."

"Please, please tell me he is also on the way back," Lydia pleaded. A dark dread came over her, and a tear slowly rolled down her cheek as reality overcame her hope.

Jacob lowered his head, slowly shaking it and holding her hands even tighter.

"I'm so, so sorry, Lydia. Another man could not have endured all he faced and survived for as long as he did. Wanting to get back to you kept him going day after day. I was there when he slowly let go of his last breath, and I helped remove him from the darkness and despair of that terrible place."

Lydia's eyes rolled back in her head, and her knees buckled. She sat down on the stone wall, trying to catch her breath.

Jacob knelt in front of her and went on. "This was a remarkable man, a patriot in every sense of the word. He sacrificed for others and was relentless in maintaining his principles of helping others. His sense of duty was unlike anything I've ever seen. It was an honor to know him for the brief time that I did."

None of what she was hearing surprised Lydia. The things that she had loved most about Samuel were his compassion, the way he showed how much he cared, and his sincerity and concern for others. But now he was gone.

CHAPTER 36

She looked into Jacob's eyes, her own flowing with tears, and thanked him for the kind words about her beloved. "When you get home, please make sure your loved ones know how much you treasure them," she told him. "In a brief time, I've lost my father, my oldest brother, and now the love of my life. It all happens so quickly and is so final. Try to make each day a moment to remember." She patted his hands as she let go. "Have a safe journey home."

He again told her he was sorry, mounted his horse, and left her alone on the wall.

Lydia sat there, sobbing heavily, for quite some time. She remembered the heartache she had felt when her father died, the deeper and more intense pain of losing Nathaniel, and now the almost unbearable sense of loss, loneliness, and heartbreak after hearing about Samuel. How could she go on?

Eventually, Lydia slowly stood up, gathered her basket of flowers, and made the slow walk—which now seemed so much longer—back to the house to give the news to her family. Everything around her at that moment seemed empty and meaningless.

Her mother was waiting outside the front door, having seen Lydia talking to the young man along the road. As Lydia approached the house, her mother noticed the despair on her face and her streaming tears.

"Lydia, my dear, what is it?" she asked.

"He's gone, Mother. My beloved Samuel is gone!"

She dropped the basket of flowers and fell into her mother's arms, sobbing uncontrollably.

*****

The sadness, despair, and uncertainty of loss felt magnified by the darkness and solitude of night as Lydia laid sleepless that night. When morning came, she gathered her thoughts and went to find her mother. Mrs. Mulliken was on a bench outside in the garden, carefully stitching a damaged quilt. Lydia sat down next to her, with her mother's arm around her, like when Lydia was very little. It gave her some comfort as she grieved over the news about Samuel.

"I know this doesn't make it easier, dear, but I understand your pain. When your father passed away, I thought my world had ended.

We had shared only a few of the many years we had expected to have together, yet they were so wonderful." Her mother stroked her hair as she spoke.

"I always admired you for being so strong when he died," Lydia said. "You held us together as a family despite your loss. What gave you the strength to go on?"

"My strength came from your father's love, a love that remained even after he was gone. Something that special stays with you, even as life moves on. I also had my faith, and each of you to care for and to remind me of him. Someday you'll understand—a mother is always thinking about others before herself."

"Samuel and I had so many dreams, and we just wanted to share our lives together forever. There has been so much loss during this war. Maybe I've become numb, but I somehow understand that someday I might be able to leave him behind and go on with my life. But he'll always be part of me and have a very special place in my heart. I survived Father's passing when I was very young, and losing Nathaniel. Maybe I'll be able to share my life with someone else someday, but that part of me will always be Samuel's and his alone."

She laid her head on her mother's shoulder and wept.

The next day, Lydia decided it was important to let the Prescotts know the news about Samuel. She asked Mary and Elijah to take her to their house in Concord, knowing the visit was not going to be as pleasant and warm as the many times she had been there previously with Samuel.

As Elijah pulled his wagon up to the edge of the Prescott property, Benjamin was coming out of their barn. He was pleased when he saw Lydia approaching. Elijah and Mary stayed in the carriage to wait for Lydia as she walked up to meet Benjamin.

"Lydia, what a welcome surprise," he said, walking over to meet her. "It's been over three years since I last saw you."

"It seems like the time has gone by much too fast, Benjamin," Lydia replied. "But I'm not here with good news for you and your family."

Benjamin stopped in his tracks, sensing her despair as her voice cracked with each word.

CHAPTER 36

"Oh no," he said, expecting her demeanor could only mean bad news about his younger brother, Samuel. "What has happened?"

Lydia stood near him with her left arm extended to caress his right shoulder. "I was told by a man returning from Canada that Samuel passed away while on a prison ship, almost a year ago. The man had been a fellow prisoner with Samuel. I felt it was so important to let your parents know."

Benjamin looked down at the ground, speaking very quietly as he told her, "My mother died last year, never the same after Abel had passed. She never recovered after losing him and then having Samuel go away." He took a deep breath, then continued. "We have to tell my father."

Lydia nodded. "We can do it together," she said while placing her arm inside his and trying to comfort him. "Take me to him."

They walked into the front door of the house, turning into the main room on the right, a room that Lydia had enjoyed during her many visits. It had always been such a pleasant room to sit in, with comfortable chairs and warm quilts; the room had always been bright, with sunlight coming through the front windows. Fresh flowers that were always on the fireplace mantle usually filled the room with a pleasant fragrance.

Lydia noticed immediately upon entering the room that there were no longer flowers on the mantle. The curtains were drawn, leaving the room darker than she remembered. She dreaded the conversation she was about to have with Samuel's father.

Dr. Abel Prescott Sr., patriarch of the family, had heard the door open and walked in from a hallway. He knew instantly from Benjamin's solemn expression and the welling of tears in Lydia's eyes that it was not just a social visit.

"Is it Samuel?" he asked, already knowing something was wrong.

"Dr. Prescott, I'm so very sorry to be the bearer of this terrible news, but yes. Samuel died last year while a prisoner in Halifax." Lydia wiped a tear that rolled down her cheek.

Dr. Prescott dropped into one of the chairs, rubbing the back of his neck with his right hand and shaking his head. "Will this rebellion ever stop hurting us?" he asked. "First Abel Jr., then my wife

Abigail, now my youngest son. I'm sorry for you as well, Lydia. I know how much you meant to each other, and we were looking forward to you becoming part of our family." His son, Benjamin, stood next to him, trying to console him.

"I share your pain, sir," Lydia said. "I lost my older brother during the siege of Boston, have two brothers out in the colonies somewhere, hopefully safe, and now my love and my future have been taken away."

"You'll always be welcome here, dear," the older Prescott assured her. "My daughter, Lucy, has married and moved away, but please feel free to come and visit at any time. We would enjoy spending some time with you sharing memories of Samuel."

Lydia turned to leave, but the doctor stood up and asked her to wait. He left the room, went into the back of the house, and retuned with a leather pouch wrapped in twine.

"I have something for you. A few times over the past couple of years, we've had a courier drop off a package that came on behalf of Samuel. In the original package, Samuel had included a note stating that he would be forwarding earnings from a new adventure that were to be kept until he returned. I believe this was intended to help the two of you start a life together. Here, this is yours." He handed Lydia the pouch. She opened it and was stunned to see a large amount of currency.

"No, no, Dr. Prescott. I can't take this," she insisted.

"You must, dear. It was intended for you and was a gift from my son. And I apologize if my mentioning Lucy's wedding was insensitive with the loss you are feeling."

"Oh no, sir. I'm so happy for her and wish her the best. But I feel uncomfortable taking this money."

"Don't feel like that—it belongs to you," the doctor said, trying to ease the awkward way she was feeling.

Lydia looked at him, then at Benjamin, and didn't know what to say.

"Take it, Lydia," Benjamin said. "Samuel would want you to use it to build your future."

CHAPTER 36

"Thank you both," she said. "I'll find a way to use it to remember him."

She turned to leave, looking back one more time, saying, "Thank you for everything."

She walked out to where Elijah and Mary were waiting. Mary asked, "Are you all right? That must have been very difficult."

"It was so hard, Mary, but they needed to know. They are wonderful people."

Elijah turned the carriage around, and they headed back to Lexington. No one spoke on the way back as the somber mood of the moment overwhelmed them all.

PART 5

On the Road to Liberty

Chapter 37

Late summer 1780

John Mulliken really disliked traveling alone. He had enjoyed having an older brother and two older sisters who he could lean on while growing up, as well as two younger brothers and a younger sister who he helped guide through the hardships of losing their father when he was only thirteen. John was used to being with others and sharing sometimes difficult experiences. As the middle child, he had always been in the middle of something. But now, after being enlisted for five years in the Continental Army and having been discharged, he was happy and relieved to be going home. John realized it meant traveling alone and knowing the house which he had grown up in was gone, but the family he loved was still there. He had seen his brother Sam just briefly in the early part of their enlistments, but their regiments were split up, and they were separated. He hoped he would see him soon.

Crossing the New York line and passing through Williamstown, John followed the trail along the Deerfield River and made it as far as Pittsfield his first day, without any difficulty. He had been given an old painted horse by a farmer in New York in appreciation for his service in the army, and it made the trip easier and much faster. He let the older horse set its own pace, even though John was anxious to get home. The horse was a little overweight, with brown and tan splotches on a palette of white on his legs, rump, and neck, a tan mane and tail. Being alone made John more aware of his surroundings, and he thought it would be safer if he kept his musket loaded

CHAPTER 37

just in case he ran into problems—either from human or wildlife confrontations. He traveled only in daylight to help reduce the chances of any wildlife issues. His plan was to proceed from Pittsfield into north central Massachusetts, passing through Fitchburg, then going through Townsend and Groton by afternoon, and reaching Lexington late in the day.

As John approached the Fitchburg area on his last day on the road, he stopped by a stream to have a quick meal and give the horse a short rest. Letting the horse graze on some grass along the gravel road, John pulled a piece of dried meat from his saddlebag and carried his wooden canteen over to a stream running alongside the trail. He sat on a rock along the edge of the stream as it slowly meandered through the countryside. As he ate, John was entertained by a pair of black-and-white dragonflies floating along the sides of the road, turning abruptly and then dipping as they scouted the area for food. From a section of lily pads in the stream below him a large bullfrog croaked its displeasure with his intrusion into their peaceful setting. A hummingbird darting between bunches of pink speedwell lining the water caught his eye. After years of battles, stress, and overcrowded camps, this quiet was just what John needed. He could have stayed there all day, but he wanted to complete the journey and get home before dark. Walking back to his horse, he drank the last of the water from the canteen, mounted his ride, and headed out.

While John was traveling through the colony, there was much happening in Lexington.

The town had offered to help Mrs. Mulliken and her children rebuild their home on the lot where it had been burned down. The Mullikens were aided by the money that Lydia had been given by the Prescotts, which had been sent through Morgan Willis, proceeds from Samuel. Myles and Elijah had organized a building party of men from Lexington and Woburn, and they had been setting the lumber in place all summer. It was nearing completion late one afternoon when the family came to check on its progress. Mrs. Mulliken sat on their stone wall along the front of the property, admiring the work, with her daughters, Mary and Lydia, standing beside her. Rebeckah was sitting on the ground in front of her, still doing her crewels.

Joseph was running between the men; now almost fifteen, he wanted to do his part and was dragging large posts and beams along the site. He struggled to lift one of the posts.

A familiar voice from the roadway caught Lydia's attention. "I think that young man needs some help," they heard him say.

Turning to see who was speaking, Lydia was surprised and yelled, "John! Mother, it's John!" She ran to embrace her brother. Her two sisters joined her. John hugged them all then walked over to his mother, dropping his hat at her feet and bending and kissing her on the forehead.

"My dear son, I'm so glad you are home," she said, tears welling in her eyes. "We have all missed you so much."

"I never thought today would come," John said, sitting on the ground beside her. "It has been a long time since I left. I've seen many horrors and pain, but it is behind me now. Sam and I both couldn't wait to head back."

"Is he all right?" Mary asked.

"He was the last time I saw him, but we were sent to different parts of the colonies. I hope he'll be returning soon safe as well."

He stood and started looking around at the work being done. "So good to see the house being brought back to life. And young Joseph has grown since I left," John said, pointing at his brother. "But where is Nathaniel? Is he inside?"

Lydia put both hands to her mouth and gasped. "You don't know?" she whispered. "He's gone, John. He died just a few months after you left just as the siege of Boston was ending."

"No! Please don't tell me that. It can't be true," John moaned. He walked out onto the road, shaking his head, his hands interlocked on top of his head. Turning back toward Lydia, he said, "I have to see him."

"But he's gone, John," Lydia repeated.

"I have to see him. Where is he?" John demanded.

Mary spoke up, "He's buried in the Old Burial Ground near Father."

"Lydia, will you go with me?" he asked.

"Of course, my dear brother."

CHAPTER 37

They walked into the center of town, Lydia putting her arm around her grieving brother. John was very disconsolate, and she tried to comfort him. He looked so sad. When they crossed the Green, he paused to look at the area where he and Nathaniel had stood together that fateful April morning. Then they slowly walked into the cemetery, and Lydia pointed out Nathaniel's stone, a tall, thin gray slate, in a row of many similar markers.

John knelt in front of the cold slate stone, his left hand resting on top while his right hand covered his heart. He stayed there without making a sound for several minutes with his head bowed. Lydia stood behind him, a steady flow of tears running down her cheeks.

Finally, he used his right hand to softly trace the engraving of Nathaniel's name in the stone, and after gently caressing the angel wings engraved in the top curve of the stone, he turned and hugged his sister. "We can go now," he whispered.

As they started walking back toward where the house was being built, John looked around town, feeling he was finally home again. He spoke softly to Lydia as they walked. "We all had such expectations of spending so many years together," he said. "Nathaniel and I always thought we would grow Father's clock business, getting Sam involved as well. The three Mulliken brothers, all working together, and in time even having young Joseph involved. We could all enjoy our own families growing together." He shook his head sadly then asked, "By the way, I haven't had the chance to ask you. Have you heard from Dr. Prescott?"

He could immediately see the answer in her face; she almost turned pale, and the tears that had finally dried on her cheeks started flowing again. Speaking very softly, Lydia looked into her brother's eyes, saying, "I was told two years ago by a man passing through town that my Samuel had died while a prisoner in Halifax. It's still painful to talk about. I miss him dearly."

John put his arms around her. "We've all paid dearly for this fight for freedom. I hope in the future we can all see it was worth it. I'm so sorry."

She rested her head on his shoulder as they finished their walk back to the house. At home, the family gathered as one, sharing in

John's return. They reflected on the sadness they had all suffered through for years and were now looking forward to moving on with their lives.

Chapter 38

November 1780

At dawn on the first morning of November, a farmer in western Massachusetts finished packing a wagon of winter vegetables and livestock for a trip to the Boston markets. The squash, turnips, and carrots were piled in the rear of the wagon, after a few chickens and two hogs were caged and placed in the front. The man climbed onto the seat of the wagon and started his day-long journey eastward.

Halfway through the day, as the fully loaded wagon rumbled across the gravel road, the farmer approached a young soldier in an old, dirty blue Continental Army uniform, trudging along the Boston-Worcester Post Road. He looked like he had been walking a long distance as his shoes were worn. His coat was torn and tattered and his trousers splattered with mud. He had a woolen scarf wrapped around his face to shelter him from the cold wind. The butt end of his musket was resting on his left shoulder.

"Young man, where are you headed?" the farmer asked as he pulled his wagon up to the soldier.

"Lexington, sir. On my way home."

"Hop on. I am passing through Lexington on my way to Boston. I'd be glad to give you a ride, as long as you don't mind sharing it with the hogs and chickens in back."

"No problem. Can't be any worse than some of the men I've been camping with for years." The soldier put his musket on top of a pile of winter squash and climbed onto the back of the wagon.

As the farmer snapped the reins to get his horses moving, he yelled back to the soldier, "What is your name, son?"

"Sam. Sam Mulliken," said the soldier. He laid back and settled down for the ride, glad to get his feet some rest.

As the sun began to descend on the horizon, the wagon pulled into Lexington center. The farmer stopped the wagon and yelled back to Sam, who had slept for the past two hours, "Mr. Mulliken, time to get off."

Sam pulled himself up, climbed off the wagon, grabbed his musket, and walked to the front of the wagon. "Thank you, sir, for your kindness." He shook the farmer's hand.

"No, young man, thank you for your service. All of us common folk owe all of the men who served our gratitude. Godspeed as you finish your journey." He gave his horses the command to continue and headed out of town.

Looking over the Green, Sam felt relieved to finally be back home. He walked over to Buckman Tavern, hoping he might find someone who could help him get to the Bagley house to reunite with his family. As he reached the door, he heard a familiar "Hah!" coming from inside. It brought a smile to his face.

Inside Buckman's, Myles Latham, Elijah Sanderson, and Joseph Burrill were finishing some ale at one of the tables in the taproom. Joseph had come into town to bring both men some leather aprons and gloves from his tannery, and Myles had offered to buy them both a drink before Joseph headed back to Haverhill. They were sitting just inside the door when a surprise visitor walked in.

"Sam Mulliken? Is that really you? Hah!" shouted Myles when he recognized Sam.

Elijah was just as pleased to see his old friend. "So good to see you again, Sam. Welcome home."

He introduced Sam to Joseph.

"Nice to meet you, Sam. I knew your father and late brother, Nathaniel."

Those words caught Sam off guard. He was glad to see friendly faces, but the news about Nathaniel was unexpected. "My late brother Nathaniel? What happened?"

CHAPTER 38

Myles stood up and put his arm around Sam. "Your brother died from disease during the siege of Boston. He is buried next to your father in the Old Burying Ground."

Sam's chin dropped as he heard the terrible news. "After all the misery and suffering that I've seen in the past six years, I had hoped my two brothers would be spared. What about my brother John? Has he returned yet?"

Elijah nodded. "Yes, he came home last month. You need to get home and see all of them. They will be so pleased."

"I've traveled so far but need a ride to the Bagley house. It's been so long since I left."

"Hah! You don't have to. Your old house was rebuilt this year. It is just up the road," Myles said, gesturing toward the edge of town. "Your family is all there."

"I want to see my brother's grave before I go." He turned to leave, but Elijah had one more piece of information. "One other bit of tragic news—Lydia's fiancée, Samuel, was also lost during the war."

"Dear Lord, does it go on forever?" Sam shook his head and left the tavern. He walked over to the Old Burying Ground to see Nathaniel's grave. The few remaining rays of sunlight on the horizon behind him cast his shadow over the headstones of both his brother and father as he stood, hat in hand, with his head bowed.

He put his hat back on and crossed the Green, heading toward the house. Sam was almost running as he got closer, anxious to finally be home. As he reached the house, he peered into one of the windows and saw the family sitting at the table, having supper. He walked to the door, knocked, and stood back when he heard the latch being lifted.

"Do you have room for a hungry soldier?" he asked as John opened the door.

His brother was so happy to see him he jumped out of the door and gave him a hug. "Sam, welcome home!" Then John called out to everyone else.

"Look what I found outside, everybody," John said.

Mrs. Mulliken ran to Sam and caressed his face to make sure she was really seeing him there. "I'm so glad you are home, my son."

"Elijah told me about Nathaniel. And, Lydia, he also told me about Samuel. I'm so sorry."

Lydia hugged him. "Thank you, Sam."

Mary came over and hugged him. Joseph stood in front of him, smiling.

Sam looked at him, surprised at how much he had grown. "Little brother? I guess I can't call you that any longer. You're so tall."

"I did what you asked me, Sam. As the man of the house after you left, I helped us all get through some rough times."

"And you did a wonderful job, Joseph."

Then Sam saw Rebeckah, standing back, waiting until everyone else was done welcoming Sam home. He walked up to her and, from his coat pocket, took out a small piece of fabric, placing it into her hands. "Rebeckah, you've become such a young lady. I have something for you. I kept this with me every day. It's a little dirty, somewhat tattered, and worn, but it was something special to remind me of home."

Rebeckah opened her hands and looked at what he had given her. It was the piece of crewel work she had given him the day he had left. She threw her arms around his neck, and everyone joined them in a family embrace.

Mrs. Mulliken looked at them and said, "Now this is one of the good days. No, a *very, very* good day."

CHAPTER 39

Winter 1781 to Spring 1782

A year later, following the victory of the colonial forces at Yorktown in October 1781, the War for Independence finally ended. The peace treaty would not be signed for another year, but the battles in the former colonies were ending. In the months to follow, those who had served began to return home throughout the colonies, and those who had tried so hard to maintain a normal life welcomed them, so happy that they were home.

In Concord the town slowly began returning to life as it had been before the war. Merchants reopened shops, and the inns and taverns became busier. Cabinetmakers, furniture makers, and chandlers started producing and selling their goods again. A key participant of the early morning of April 19, 1775, Amos Melvin, who rang the alarm bell after hearing the warning from Samuel on that fateful night, welcomed two sons during the war. He was so impressed with his memory of the fast response to the alarm by Reverend William Emerson, and the reverend's passion and commitment, he named his first two sons William and Emerson.

The village of Lexington, as well, saw the return of many of the men who had left to fight for freedom. The farms that had slowed down or gone dormant sprang back to life. Blacksmiths, tanners, carpenters, and even clockmakers returned to their trades. John Mulliken continued to stay in town, later married a young lady named Lydia Whiting, and had a son; they named him Nathaniel after John's father and brother. Sam joined his brother, John, in renewing the clockmaking business. Their sister, Mary, married Elijah Sanderson, who eventually became a prominent cabinetmaker in Salem.

In both towns, and among all the colonies, it was time for life to move on. The hardship and struggles endured during the years of turmoil and conflict now blended with endless hope, and together they created people strong and resilient. Ordinary people had forged an extraordinary change in their world and for the future. These people, men and women of all ages, multiple races and nationalities, sacrificed homes, fortunes, and many times their lives in a quest for liberty and freedom. Impassioned words and promises often deeply impact those most affected, but the deeds and actions that follow define the true measure of people and leaders, many times helping to determine the end result. Yes, there were many obstacles and difficulties still ahead as they developed a new government under the recent Articles of Confederation and worked to grow their new nation, but the dignity, sacrifice, and commitment shared by the communities and the people who lived in them would carry them to a better place. The British army and loyalists were finally gone; those moving forward were now Americans.

The following spring, Lydia was still helping her mother and siblings get their lives back together. One evening, after night had fallen, she wrapped a shawl around her shoulders and went outside to help Joseph bring in some wood for the night. Several dry brown leaves, remnants of the previous fall, danced across the walkway in front of her, lifted by a warming April breeze.

"Joseph, can I help?" she asked as she approached the wood pile in back of the house.

"Sure. Can you bring in some of the kindling to help me restart the fire in the morning?" Joseph smiled at his sister.

"Gladly," she said, knowing he could have easily done that himself, but he understood that she wanted to help. "Thank you, Joseph, for always being so kind and helpful."

"Since John and Sam now have their own families and homes, it's my responsibility to help. I don't mind."

She put her right hand on his shoulder. "They would be so proud of their little brother. I know you miss them all."

CHAPTER 39

"I just want to be as good a provider as Nathaniel was," Joseph replied.

"You're doing a fine job," Lydia told him. She realized for the first time he was now taller than she was.

Joseph picked up several logs and carried the wood toward the house, stopping briefly to look back over his left shoulder at his sister. Seeing her gazing up at the night sky, he asked, "Lydia, are you all right?"

"Yes, I am, Joseph. Thank you for caring."

He smiled back at her sheepishly and continued into the house with an armload of firewood.

As Lydia gathered a handful of smaller oak and maple pieces inside the woodpile, she looked up again at the darkening sky. What a beautiful night it was! Every star seemed to jump out of the clear sky. She paused briefly, and her eyes began to water as her memory of Samuel sharing the large rock that night so long ago flashed through her mind. Over the years, she had often looked up at the stars, hoping he was somewhere doing the same thing; now she hoped he was looking down at her. "I hope you are watching over me, my love," she said to herself. A slight smile crossed her face, showing both joy and much pain, and a single tear slowly ran down her left cheek.

Lydia turned, took one more glance at the black sky with the sprinkling of glittering silver stars, and headed inside.

PART 6

Additional Information

APPENDIX 1

Dedication/Acknowledgments

This story is dedicated to the men, women, and families of *both* sides, and their allies, who only wanted what was best for them and their future. Their sacrifice, determination, and commitment throughout the time period deserve our respect and admiration.

Special thanks are owed to my two daughters, Tara and Caitlyn, for their support in this effort. They helped edit my ideas and thoughts, encouraged me throughout the process, and always accepted my sometime intense love of history. They made more than one 5:00 a.m. trip to see the Lexington reenactment.

I mostly want to thank my wife, Carol, for her support and for spending all these years sharing my passion for Revolutionary War history. The countless trips to historic sites, museums, libraries, bookstores, and even cemeteries were more enjoyable because she was there to share them with me. Our many walks over the North Bridge and other sites in Boston, Concord, Lincoln, and Lexington were very special. We didn't make history, but we made lifelong memories that we will forever cherish. Her patience, understanding, and support over the twenty years it took for me to complete this story, including the many hours after dinner that I spent writing/editing/revising are so appreciated.

Appendix 2

Points of Interest

Interested in bringing some of this story to life? Visit these spots and see some of the actual locations and items described in these pages.

- Lexington Green, Lexington, Massachusetts (including monument for eight men killed on the green; a replica of the old Belfry Tower is on a hill nearby)
- Buckman Tavern, Lexington, Massachusetts—next to Lexington Green
- Jonathan Harrington House, Lexington, Massachusetts (now private residence)
- William Diamond's drum can be seen at Buckman Tavern
- Munroe Tavern, Lexington, Massachusetts—east of the center of Lexington—includes a display that has spoons that had been hidden by the Mullikens before house was burned down and a Mulliken tall clock.
- Old Burial Ground, Lexington—stones marking the graves of Nathaniel Mulliken, all six of the Childs' children; John Mulliken and his wife, Lydia Whiting, are also there at the other end, as are many of the Lexington people mentioned in the story; also graves of British soldiers.

- Plaque showing site of Percy's cannons and Mulliken House, Lexington, Massachusetts
- Major Pitcairn's pistols, Munroe Tavern, Lexington, Massachusetts (After he lost them, they were given to Israel Putnam, who used them throughout the war; some recent insight claims they may have belonged to another soldier from Crosbie family.)
- Wright's Tavern, Concord, Massachusetts
- The Old Manse (Reverend William Emerson's house), Concord, Massachusetts
- Meriam House, Concord, Massachusetts
- Barrett's Farm, Concord, Massachusetts
- North Bridge, Concord, Massachusetts (including gravesite of two British soldiers who died there)
- Major Buttrick's House, Concord, Massachusetts
- John Hancock trunk and one of Revere's signal lanterns, Concord Museum, Concord, Massachusetts
- Mulliken Clock from Buckman Tavern, Concord Museum, Concord, Massachusetts
- Dr. Minot's Liberty Tavern, now part of Colonial Inn, Concord, Massachusetts
- Battle Road, from Lexington to Concord—Parker's Revenge site, Revere capture site, the
- Captain William Smith House (commander of Lincoln militia and brother of Abigail Adams), remains of Hartwell House, Hartwell Tavern, Brooks Houses.
- Hill Burial Ground, Concord, Massachusetts—where Pitcairn and Smith stood upon entering town.
- Plaque showing site of Samuel Prescott's House, Concord, Massachusetts
- Robbins Farm marker, Acton, Massachusetts—shows where Captain Robbins house stood
- Davis Farm marker, Acton, Massachusetts—shows where Isaac Davis house stood
- Bunker Hill Monument, Charlestown, Massachusetts

APPENDIX 2

- Kendall Tavern, Dunstable, Massachusetts (now a private residence)
- Bunker Hill Memorial Bench, Pepperell, Massachusetts
- Daughters of the American Revolution Boulder honoring where William Prescott and Pepperell men gathered, Pepperell, Massachusetts
- Stone commemorating Prudence Wright and her band of women who captured British couriers at Prudence Wright Overlook, next to restored covered bridge, Pepperell, Massachusetts
- Major John Pitcairn Burial Vault, Old North Church, Boston, Massachusetts (also site of signal lanterns alarming Paul Revere of the route being taken by the Regulars on April 19)
- Fitch Tavern, Bedford, Massachusetts—still has original tavern, but house is private residence.
- Moffatt/Ladd House, Portsmouth, New Hampshire (William Whipple tree/damask rose still there)
- Fort Ticonderoga, Ticonderoga, New York; the Knox Trail that Henry Knox took transporting the cannons to Boston is marked by fifty-six markers, starting at Crown Point, New York, and ending in Roxbury, Massachusetts
- And of course, Freedom Trail in Boston, including Boston Massacre marker.
- One additional point of interest—Halifax was the site of British evacuation from Boston and the unmarked grave of Dr. Samuel Prescott. In a strange twist of fate, in 1917, when a munitions ship in Halifax Harbor exploded, destroying much of the city, Boston came to their aid with food, water, and medical assistance. This created a strong relationship that is reflected in the annual donation by Halifax of a large Christmas tree used on Boston Common each Christmas.

Appendix 3

Characters Created

The following characters were not real people of the time but added to help build the story and fill in places and events not documented.

- Isaac, Sarah and Jacob Walker
- Hastings (Pitcairn's aide)
- Patrick Barnicle
- John Masters
- David Quimby
- Myles and Prudence Latham
- The Bagleys
- Matthew Willis
- Seth Taylor
- Greydon Pike
- Morgan Willis
- Maxwell Dodd
- Captain Peter Lucas Grant
- Crew of the *Gryphon*
- Stella Fairweather (actual person but from another time—my maternal grandmother)
- Augustine Scott

APPENDIX 3

- Commander Clark Morris
- Mr. Abernathy

The names of horses used (Duchess, Rascal, etc.) were also created. All other characters were real-life participants.

APPENDIX 4

Suggested Reading

Interested in reading more about the actual historical events and participants? Here are some great books that inspired me. Enjoy!

Arthur B. Tourtellot, *Lexington and Concord;* W.W. Norton & Company, Inc., 1959

Originally published as *William Diamond's Drum,* this book offers many details and stories that catch the reader's attention; this book was a main inspiration.

David Hackett Fischer, *Paul Revere's Ride;* Oxford University Press, 1994

Tremendous account of Paul Revere's ride and surrounding events; well researched and well written, easy to read.

Thomas Fleming, *Now We Are Enemies;* American History Press, 2010 (Anniversary Edition)

One of the most detailed description of events and activities of the Breed's Hill battle and those who were there. Great narrative of all aspects of the battle and participants.

APPENDIX 4

Fred J. Cook, *Privateers of '76:* The Boobs-Merrill Company, Inc., 1976
Historical description of the men and ships that worked the seas for the colonies.

Charles J. Caes, *Legend of the Third Horseman;* Xlibris Books, 2009
A different perspective on Samuel Prescott's participation and motivations.

J. L. Bell, *The Road to Concord;* Westholme Publishing, 2016
Narrative that details the discovery of weapons and supplies being hidden by militia through British spies and events that followed.

Phillip S. Greenwalt and Robert Orrison, *A Single Blow;* Savas Beatie, 2018
Good book that focuses on early battles and beginning of the Revolution, part of a series on the Emerging Revolutionary War.

Charles H. Bradford, M.D., *The Battle Road;* The Rotary Club of Boston, 1975
Interesting booklet that covers all the activities along Battle Road on the days before, during, and after April 19.

Albert Greene, *Recollections of the Jersey Prison Ship;* H.H. Brown, 1829
Information from memoirs and observations from prisoners and others regarding a prison ship in New York Harbor that details the deplorable conditions.

Thomas Fleming, *Liberty! The American Revolution;* Viking/Penguin Group, 1977
For anyone interested in the entire scope of the War for Independence. This classic covers the full scope of the war.

David McCullough, *1776;* Simon and Schuster, 2005

An interesting and detailed description of the basis for events in 1776, especially activities of many of the military and political leaders.

John Greenwood, *A Young Patriot in the American Revolution;* Westvaco, 1989
Firsthand accounts of life as a Continental soldier.

William Pierce Randel, *Mirror of a People;* Hamond, 1973
Great introduction to culture and daily lives of colonial America with an abundance of informative pictures.

Esmond Wright, *The Fire of Liberty;* The Folio Society, 1983
British perspective of the American War of Independence; interesting to see it from the English point of view.

The American Heritage Book of the American Revolution; American Heritage Publishing, 1958
An older but useful and inspiring book that details the events and people who were part of the building of our nation.

Bart McDowell, *The Revolutionary War;* The National Geographic Society, 1967
Both an historic and geographic telling of the Revolution using places, events and the people involved.

There are also some wonderful special excerpts published by the Boston Globe in 1975 for the Bicentennial on both Lexington/Concord (March, 1975) and Breed's Hill (May, 1975).

In addition, *Discover Concord* (Voyager Publishing), a high-quality quarterly magazine, usually has some interesting and informative articles on Concord history in each issue, often dealing with something from the Revolutionary times. They also did a great article on descendants of Amos Melvin, the three Melvin brothers who died during the Civil War and are memorialized with a magnificent memorial sculpture requested by their brother James; it is in

APPENDIX 4

Sleepy Hollow Cemetery in Concord. The memorial was designed and made by Daniel Chester French, who also did the Minute Man statue near Concord's North Bridge, and Lincoln statue at Lincoln Memorial in Washington, DC.

About the Author

Gary Entwistle is a graduate of UMASS Lowell with a bachelor of arts degree in history/political science. This is Gary's first book, the culmination of a twenty-year labor of love, put on hold several times to help his wife raise two intelligent and independent daughters and during a long, successful sales career. He was always fascinated with the War for Independence and was fortunate to live close enough to Lexington, Concord, and Boston to spend a lot of time there exploring and researching. A member of the Concord Museum and the Lexington Historical Society, his love of history and exploration of historical sites with his wife, Carol, is surpassed only by their love of gardens, family, and the wonders of the southern coast of Maine and mountains of Vermont.

CPSIA information can be obtained
at www.ICGtesting.com
Printed in the USA
JSHW031410200522
26061JS00001B/11